JOURNEYS

Reader's Notebook

Grade 4

HOUGHTON MIFFLIN HARCOURT

School Publishers

Contents

Unit 4

Unit 5

Unit 6

Name _____ Date _____

Lesson 2
READER'S NOTEBOOK

My Brother Martin
Independent Reading

 Reader's Guide

My Brother Martin

Mother Dear, Why?

Christine writes about growing up with her famous brother, Martin Luther King, Jr. During the time when she and her brother were growing up, certain historical events influenced their lives. Think about details in the text to help you understand the historical events.

Read page 55. M. L. and A. D. came alone that day. Think about why they came home alone.

What did their playmates tell them?

_____

_____

_____

_____

Think about the historical events during the time. What allowed their playmates to treat M. L. and A. D. this way?

_____

_____

_____

_____

Independent Reading
13
Grade 4, Unit 1

Read pages 56–57. M. L. finally asks his mother, "Why do white people treat colored people so mean?" What do you think Mother Dear says? Write her answer in her words. Make sure to include details about the historical events that caused colored people to be treated so unfairly.

Prefixes *in-*, *im-*, *il-*, and *ir-*

injustice   irresponsible   impolite   insecure
illegal   imperfect   irreplaceable

Read each underlined word. Use the meaning of the prefix to help you understand the meaning of the word. Then complete the sentence in a way that makes sense.

1. I know I am <u>irresponsible</u> when I

_____ .

2. It is <u>impolite</u> to

_____ .

3. The law says it is <u>illegal</u> to

_____ .

4. I feel <u>insecure</u> when I

_____ .

5. The <u>imperfect</u> pair of pants had

_____ .

6. Losing something that is <u>irreplaceable</u>

_____ .

7. One example of an <u>injustice</u> is

_____ .

Short *e* and Long *e*

Basic 1–11.   Write the Basic Word that best fits each clue.

1. inexpensive _____

2. a desire for more than one needs

   _____

3. a large animal _____

4. direction where the Sun sets _____

5. shine brightly _____

6. a small spot _____

7. rising at a very sharp angle _____

8. leader _____

9. water in the form of a gas _____

10. to think _____

11. a place for books or other items _____

Challenge 12–14.   Write a paragraph about a place where you like to go to eat. Tell what you like about it. Use three Challenge Words. Write on a separate sheet of paper.

Spelling Words

1. west
2. steep
3. member
4. gleam
5. fresh
6. freedom
7. speed
8. steam
9. beast
10. believe
11. speck
12. kept
13. cheap
14. pretend
15. greed
16. shelf
17. least
18. eager
19. reason
20. chief

Challenge
echo
menu
creature
reveal
restaurant

Spelling Word Sort

Write each Basic Word beside the correct heading.

/ĕ/ spelled *e* followed by a consonant	Basic Words: Challenge Words: Possible Selection Words:
/ē/ spelled *ea*	Basic Words: Challenge Words: Possible Selection Words:
/ē/ spelled *ee*	Basic Words: Possible Selection Words:
Other spellings for /ē/	Basic Words:

Spelling Words

1. west
2. steep
3. member
4. gleam
5. fresh
6. freedom
7. speed
8. steam
9. beast
10. believe
11. speck
12. kept
13. cheap
14. pretend
15. greed
16. shelf
17. least
18. eager
19. reason
20. chief

Challenge

echo
menu
creature
reveal
restaurant

Challenge Add the Challenge Words to your Word Sort.

Connect to Reading Look through "My Brother Martin." Find words that have the /ĕ/ or /ē/ sounds. Add them to your Word Sort.

Proofreading for Spelling

My Brother Martin
Spelling: Short *e* and Long *e*

Find the misspelled words and circle them. Write them correctly on the lines below.

Many years ago, Africans were forced to come to the United States as slaves. They lived without fredom. Many people were against slavery. They, at leest, were eagre to spead change and worked hard to free slaves.

Slavery was abolished, but change was slow. When Dr. Martin Luther King, Jr. was a boy, his mother explained that she could no longer preten to beleeve that as a menber of the Atlanta community, she could eat at any restaurant in the city or stroll in the park and enjoy the freshh air. The reasen she gave was that some states still had unfair laws that kepp black people and white people separate.

Though Dr. King paid a steap price for working for equality, his contributions would offer a gleem of hope that change would come.

1. _____   7. _____
2. _____   8. _____
3. _____   9. _____
4. _____   10. _____
5. _____   11. _____
6. _____   12. _____

Spelling Words

1. west
2. steep
3. member
4. gleam
5. fresh
6. freedom
7. speed
8. steam
9. beast
10. believe
11. speck
12. kept
13. cheap
14. pretend
15. greed
16. shelf
17. least
18. eager
19. reason
20. chief

Challenge

echo
menu
creature
reveal
restaurant

Declarative and Interrogative Sentences

A sentence that makes a statement is a **declarative sentence**. It ends with a period. A sentence that asks a question is an **interrogative sentence**. It ends with a question mark. Every sentence begins with a capital letter.

Thinking Questions
Does the sentence make a statement? Does the sentence ask a question?

declarative sentence	**interrogative sentence**
Martin Luther King Jr. gave many speeches.	What did you learn about Dr. King?

Add the correct end punctuation. Write whether each sentence is *declarative* or *interrogative*.

1. Dr. King gave a famous speech in 1963 _____

2. Were the words "I have a dream" in the speech _____

3. Have you ever read the speech _____

4. The occasion was a march in Washington _____

5. At least 200,000 people were there _____

6. What was the speech about _____

7. How did listeners respond to the speech _____

8. Dr. King spoke of his dreams of freedom _____

9. Do you think a speech can change history _____

10. Many said it was the best speech of 20th century

   America _____

Name _____ Date _____

Imperative and Exclamatory Sentences

A sentence that gives a command is an **imperative sentence**. It ends with a period or an exclamation point. A sentence that shows strong feeling is an **exclamatory sentence**. It ends with an exclamation point.

Thinking Questions
Does the sentence give a command? Does the sentence show strong feeling?

imperative sentence
Discuss the fight for civil rights.

exclamatory sentence
What a hard struggle it was!

1–10. Add the correct end punctuation. Write *imperative* or *exclamatory*.

1. Read about special laws for African Americans _____

2. How unfair those laws were _____

3. Find out why the laws changed _____

4. Learn about freedom marches _____

5. How inspiring the marches were _____

6. Some people were so courageous _____

7. Dr. King was an awesome speaker _____

8. Imagine having thousands of people hear your words _____

9. Think about how much our country has changed _____

10. What an important part of our history _____

Four Kinds of Sentences

A **declarative sentence** makes a statement and ends with a period. An **interrogative sentence** asks a question and ends with a question mark. An **imperative sentence** gives a command and ends with a period or exclamation point. An **exclamatory sentence** shows strong feeling and ends with an exclamation point.

Thinking Questions
What is the purpose of the sentence? What punctuation should be used?

Washington has many memorials.
Have you seen the Lincoln Memorial?
Decide what you want to see.
It will be a great trip!

Add the correct end punctuation. Write whether each sentence is *declarative, interrogative, imperative,* **or** *exclamatory.*

1. Look at this picture _____

2. This is a national memorial in our nation's capital _____

3. What is the memorial's purpose _____

4. Martin Luther King Jr., is honored _____

5. Some quotes by Dr. King are on a wall _____

6. Isn't there a statue of Dr. King _____

7. Try to go see the memorial _____

8. I can't wait to see it _____

9. Should we plan to visit Dr. King's memorial together _____

10. There are many memorials in our nation's capital _____

Contractions

A **contraction** is a short way to write two words. An **apostrophe** takes the place of a letter or letters in a contraction.

contractions

She <u>will</u>	she'll
has <u>not</u>	hasn't
I <u>have</u>	I've

1–4. Write the contraction of the underlined words on the line.

1. <u>They will</u> share their stories. _____

2. Caitlin <u>should have</u> written a report. _____

3. <u>I am</u> going to write about kindness. _____

4. <u>I will</u> write a report about Dr. Martin Luther King Jr. _____

5–8. Write the words that make up the underlined contraction on the line.

5. People said that <u>they'd</u> march in the streets. _____

6. Rosa Parks <u>wouldn't</u> give up her seat on the bus. _____

7. Dr. King thought that people <u>shouldn't</u> ride the bus for a while.

_____

8. Every adult in America <u>should've</u> voted. _____

Sentence Fluency

Statements	Varying Sentence Types
There were many civil rights leaders. They had many challenges. They fought for equality. You can find out what they did.	There were many civil rights leaders. They had so many challenges! How did they fight for equality? Find out what they did.

Change each underlined statement to a question, a command, or an exclamation. The word in parentheses ( ) tells you which kind of sentence to write. Write the sentences on the lines below.

Civil rights leaders brought about change. (question) They used different methods. Lawyer Thurgood Marshall worked for civil rights. You can study Marshall's accomplishments. (imperative) They were amazing. (exclamatory)

There are ways to challenge unfair laws. (question) Thurgood Marshall challenged them in court. He had a case against a Kansas public school system. He won. (exclamatory) As a result, African-American students could attend schools with white students. President Johnson appointed Marshall to the Supreme Court in 1964. He was the first African-American Supreme Court Justice. You can remember Thurgood Marshall as a great civil rights leader. (imperative)

1. _____

2. _____

3. _____

4. _____

5. _____

6. _____

Focus Trait: Word Choice
Words That Describe

My Brother Martin
Writing: Narrative Writing

A. Read each sentence about the story. Look at the underlined words used to express feelings. Then rewrite the sentence using vivid words and details that describe.

Poor Word Choice	Vivid Word Choice
1. M. L. and A. D. <u>did not like</u> learning to play the piano.	
2. Many people <u>cared</u> about equal rights.	

B. Read each sentence about the story. Rewrite it, using vivid words that describe the characters' feelings.

Pair/Share Work with a partner to brainstorm vivid words for your sentences.

3. M. L. wanted people to treat each other better.	
4. M. L. was a kind person.	
5. M. L. admired his father's actions.	

My Librarian Is a Camel

My Library Card

Answer the questions below by rereading pages 80–81 and by looking at the photographs of "My Librarian Is a Camel."

In the picture on the left, what are the children doing?

_____

_____

_____

How are they dressed? How do they look? What does this tell you about how much they want to get their books?

_____

_____

_____

If they can use a sled all the way to the post office, what does this tell you about the area they live in?

_____

_____

_____

Independent Reading

25

Grade 4 , Unit 1

Read page 81. Think about how important the books are to the boys in Cambridge Bay, Canada. Design a library card that shows the goals of the Northwest Territories Borrower-by-Mail system. Include visuals and a slogan. A slogan is a catchy phrase that tells the goals of an organization.

Front

200000002

Back

Signature _____

Name _____ Date _____

Lesson 3
READER'S NOTEBOOK

**My Librarian Is
a Camel**
Vocabulary Strategies:
Using Context

Using Context

energetic   generous   relative   grateful
homesick   negative   thoughtful

**Complete each sentence with a word from above. Use context
clues to help you.**

1. Having his own books to read at camp kept Mark from

   getting _____ .

2. Mr. Cook's donation of 100 books to the town library was

   very _____ .

3. A library boat takes books to Uncle Niko, a _____

   of mine in Finland.

4. A camel must be very _____ to carry 400 pounds

   of books.

5. This cheerful book will get rid of _____ thoughts.

6. The residents are _____ for the workers who bring

   them books.

7. It was _____ of the librarian to save that book

   for Soren.

Short *i* and Long *i*

Basic 1–9. Read the paragraph. Write the Basic Word that best replaces the underlined word or words in the sentences.

As I walk through the zoo, I (1) <u>repeat to</u> myself to visit the new monkey house. It is made of glass and red (2) <u>hard clay block</u>. There was a damp (3) <u>coolness</u> in the old monkey house. Now the monkeys (4) <u>reside</u> in a comfortable environment. There is a (5) <u>trench</u> between the trees and the glass that separates visitors from the monkeys. As I stand outside the glass, I give a (6) <u>loud breath</u> when I don't see any monkeys. I am about to (7) <u>conclude</u> that the monkeys are not in their new home yet, when I look up in the trees. The monkeys look down at me, and I smile with (8) <u>happiness</u>. I can't wait to tell my family about my zoo visit when we have dinner (9) <u>this evening</u>.

1. _____ 6. _____

2. _____ 7. _____

3. _____ 8. _____

4. _____ 9. _____

5. _____

Challenge 10–12. Write some rules that visitors to a zoo might need to follow. Use three of the Challenge Words. Write on a separate sheet of paper.

Spelling Words

1. skill
2. crime
3. grind
4. tonight
5. brick
6. flight
7. live
8. chill
9. delight
10. build
11. ditch
12. decide
13. witness
14. wind
15. district
16. inch
17. sigh
18. fright
19. remind
20. split

Challenge
ignorant
recognize
advice
twilight
rigid

Spelling Word Sort

My Librarian Is a Camel
Spelling: Short *i* and Long *i*

Write each Basic Word beside the correct heading. You will use two Basic Words more than once.

/ ĭ / spelled *i* followed by a consonant	Basic Words: Challenge Words: Possible Selection Words:
/ ĭ / spelled *ui*	Basic Words:
/ ī / spelled *i*-consonant-*e*	Basic Words: Challenge Words: Possible Selection Words:
/ ī / spelled *igh*	Basic Words: Challenge Words: Possible Selection Words:
/ ī / spelled *i* followed by a consonant	Basic Words: Possible Selection Words:
can be pronounced / ĭ / or / ī /	Basic Words:

Spelling Words

1. skill
2. crime
3. grind
4. tonight
5. brick
6. flight
7. live
8. chill
9. delight
10. build
11. ditch
12. decide
13. witness
14. wind
15. district
16. inch
17. sigh
18. fright
19. remind
20. split

Challenge
ignorant
recognize
advice
twilight
rigid

Challenge   Add the Challenge Words to your Word Sort.

Connect to Reading   Look through *My Librarian Is a Camel*. Find words that have / ĭ / and / ī /. Add them to your Word Sort.

Proofreading for Spelling

Find the misspelled words and circle them. Write them correctly on the lines below.

For children who liv in very isolated areas, new books are a treat. They cannot visit a local library or witniss a new bookstore opening. Many communities have no resources to bild such places. So leaders must deside how to get books to the children. It would be a crimme for children to go without books.

At an airport in the Arctic, three friends wait for the mail flite to arrive. A strong wynd blows. A moment of frite passes like a cill. What if the books do not come tonite? One boy lets out a loud sie. Then the children giggle with delite as the package appears. The new books are here!

1. _____
2. _____
3. _____
4. _____
5. _____
6. _____
7. _____
8. _____
9. _____
10. _____
11. _____
12. _____

Spelling Words

1. skill
2. crime
3. grind
4. tonight
5. brick
6. flight
7. live
8. chill
9. delight
10. build
11. ditch
12. decide
13. witness
14. wind
15. district
16. inch
17. sigh
18. fright
19. remind
20. split

Challenge
ignorant
recognize
advice
twilight
rigid

Quotation Marks with Direct Speech

A **quotation** is made up of the exact words that someone has said. Use **quotation marks** (" ") before and after the quotation.

Always capitalize the first word of a quotation and use correct end punctuation. When the quotation begins a sentence, use a comma at the end of the statement unless it is a question or exclamation. If the speaker's name begins a sentence, use a comma after *said*.

quotation

"I wish we lived near a library," said Arun.

quotation

Cristo said, "I'd take home books every day if we did."

Thinking Questions
What words tell that someone is speaking? What are the exact words that person says?

Write each sentence correctly. Capitalize words that should be capitalized. Add quotation marks, commas, and end marks where they are needed.

1. The bookmobile is coming today said Katie

_____

2. Sam said I've never seen a bookmobile

_____

3. it's a big bus that takes library books to people said Katie

_____

4. Sam said let's visit the bookmobile this afternoon

_____

_____

Split Quotations

Sometimes the words that tell who is speaking come in the middle of a quotation.

If the first part of the quotation is a complete sentence, use a comma before and then a period after the words that tell who is speaking. Capitalize the first letter in the second sentence of the quotation.

Example: "I lived near the North Pole," said Dad. "There were no libraries nearby."

If the entire quotation is one sentence, use a comma after the words that tell who is speaking. Do not capitalize the first letter in the second part of the quotation.

Example: "I love to read," he said, "so I found ways to get books."

Thinking Questions
Is the quotation broken into parts? Where does the punctuation belong?

1–4.   Write the quotations correctly.

1. I read all the time exclaimed Anna it's nice to have plenty of books

_____

2. some people are not so lucky said Ms. Owens they live far from a library

_____

3. how do they get books asked Anna everyone needs books to read

_____

4. some people get books by plane said Ms. Owens and others get them by boat

_____

Quotations from Text

For a report, you might use a quotation from a text. Use the same punctuation and capitalization rules that you use for other quotations. The name of the book or author that the quotation comes from is called the source. Be sure to include the source. Be sure to use the source's exact words.

Original text: "Camels are known for their ability to survive long periods without drinking water."
Source: "The Encyclopedia of Mammals"

quotation from text:
According to "The Encyclopedia of Mammals," "Camels are known for their ability to survive long periods without drinking water."

Original text: "People use camels much as they use horses, for transportation and other hard work."
Source: author Jennet Blanes

quotation from text:
"People use camels much as they use horses, for transportation and other hard work," writes Jennet Blanes.

Thinking Questions
What are the author's exact words? Where does the punctuation belong?

1. Quotation: "Camels have been helping people for centuries."
   Source: "Animals and People, Working Together"

   _____

2. Quotation: "In Africa, camels are an important means of transportation."
   Source: author James Silter

   _____

Contractions

Two Words	Contraction
I am already homesick.	**I'm** already homesick.
We are going away for the entire summer.	**We're** going away for the entire summer.
You will have a great time.	**You'll** have a great time.

1–5. **Write the contractions for the underlined words.**

1. You are going to miss summer baseball. _____

2. I have heard that summers are hot in the islands. _____

3. My grandmother said it is hot and humid every day. _____

4. Mom said we will be close to the beach. _____

5. She is looking forward to being with my grandparents. _____

6–10. **This note has five mistakes in the use of contractions. Underline the mistakes and write the contractions correctly on the lines below.**

Hi Cody,

    Iv'e been on the island for a week, and I'm having a great
time. My cousins are so cool. Theyr'e baseball nuts, like you
and I are. W'eve bought tickets to a baseball game. I can
e-mail you some pictures. Your'e going to laugh when you
see me in the straw hat. Its going to be a great summer
after all.

                 Bye for now,
                 David

6. _____

7. _____

8. _____

9. _____

10. _____

Sentence Fluency

As you edit your writing, check for proper capitalization and punctuation of quotations. Also, make your writing more lively and precise by using different words for *said* in the words that tell who is speaking, such as *Terry said.*

A Quotation with *said*	A More Precise Word for *said*
"Maybe Lassie could take our books home on her back," Terry said.	"Maybe Lassie could take our books home on her back," Terry joked.

Rewrite each sentence. Add capital letters and punctuation. Replace *said* with a more precise word. Write the new sentence on the line.

1. our new library is awesome Jake said

   _____

2. what is the history of libraries Maria said

   _____

3. there haven't been public libraries for that long
   Ms. Chance said

   _____

   _____

4. early American towns had libraries Ms. Chance
   said it cost money to borrow books, though

   _____

   _____

5. Lucy said I'm glad we can borrow books for free now

   _____

6. Public libraries are a great resource Ms. Chance said

   _____

My Librarian Is a Camel
Writing:
Narrative Writing

Focus Trait: Voice
Informal Speech

Weak Dialogue	Informal, Natural Speech
"I very much like that book."	"That book is great!"

1–2. Read each line of dialogue. Rewrite the underlined phrases to make them sound more natural and informal.

1. "You will enjoy this book because it has many interesting characters."	"_____ this book because it has _____ characters."
2. "We can consult the librarian about worthwhile reading material for our book club."	"_____ the librarian about _____ for our book club."

3–5. Read each line of dialogue. Rewrite it to make it sound more natural.

Pair/Share   Work with a partner to brainstorm words for your dialogue.

3. "A frightening mystery story is often a popular choice."	
4. "There should be no problem locating the titles of current books on the Internet."	
5. "We can select our books based on members' recommendations."	

Reader's Guide

The Power of W.O.W.!
Actor Call!

Imagine you are the director of the play *The Power of W.O.W.!* You would like to help the actress who will play Ileana understand her character. Complete the activity to write a description that helps the actress understand her role.

Read page 113. What line of dialogue on the page tells that Ileana is committed to helping save the W.O.W. program?

_____

_____

_____

What is the stage direction for Ileana on page 116? What does the stage direction tell you about how Ileana feels about asking Uncle Carlos for a favor?

_____

_____

_____

What can you infer about Ileana's character from her words and stage direction? How does it help you understand the play's theme?

_____

_____

_____

You are the director of the play, and you are trying to help the actress playing Ileana. Write a description of the character you can give to the actress. Be sure you tell what Ileana contributes to the theme of the play.

_____

_____

_____

_____

_____

_____

_____

_____

_____

_____

_____

_____

_____

_____

_____

_____

Prefixes *non-, mis-*

misplace	mistreat	nonfiction
misspelled	misjudged	nonsense
misunderstand	nonbeliever	nonstop

Complete each phrase to make a complete sentence. In items
1–7, use your own words to complete the sentences in a way
that makes sense. In items 8–9, choose a word from the box to
complete the sentences.

1. To make sure I don't turn in an assignment with

   misspelled words, I _____ .

2. I am a nonbeliever in _____ .

3. If I misunderstand what was said, I

   _____ .

4. The most important thing I have ever misplaced was my

   _____ .

5. When you mistreat your belongings, they

   _____ .

6. My favorite nonfiction book is _____ .

7. One time I misjudged _____ .

8. My sister Tina talks _____ on her

   phone with friends from school.

9. My dad thinks that buying a new school bag every year is

   _____ .

Words with Short *o* and Long *o*

Basic 1–10. Write the Basic Word that completes each analogy.

1. *Soup* is to *lunch* as _____ is to *breakfast*.

2. *Typed* is to *e-mail* as _____ is to *letter*.

3. *Shout* is to *yell* as *brag* is to _____ .

4. *Near* is to *close* as *distant* is to _____ .

5. *Normal* is to *usual* as *strange* is to _____ .

6. *Lose* is to *lost* as _____ is to *found*.

7. *Climb* is to *hill* as _____ is to *problem*.

8. *Approve* is to *disapprove* as *praise* is to _____ .

9. *Teacher* is to *students* as _____ is to *guests*.

10. *Surf* is to *wave* as *ski* is to _____ .

Challenge 11–14. Write a paragraph about taking an ocean voyage to another country. Tell about your trip on the ocean. Use four of the Challenge Words. Write on a separate sheet of paper.

Spelling Words

1. block
2. shown
3. oatmeal
4. wrote
5. fellow
6. scold
7. coast
8. odd
9. locate
10. slope
11. throat
12. host
13. online
14. shock
15. solve
16. known
17. remote
18. stock
19. boast
20. globe

Challenge
bonus
approach
motion
continent
accomplish

Spelling Word Sort

Write each Basic Word beside the correct heading.

/ŏ/ spelled *o* followed by a consonant	Basic Words: Challenge Words: Possible Selection Words:
/ō/ spelled *o*-consonant-*e*	Basic Words: Possible Selection Words:
/ō/ spelled *oa*	Basic Words: Challenge Words:
/ō/ spelled *ow*	Basic Words: Possible Selection Words:
/ō/ spelled *o* followed by a consonant	Basic Words: Challenge Words: Possible Selection Words:

Challenge   Add the Challenge Words to your Word Sort.

Connect to Reading   Look through "The Power of W.O.W.!" Find words that have /ŏ/ and /ō/. Add them to your Word Sort.

Spelling Words

1. block
2. shown
3. oatmeal
4. wrote
5. fellow
6. scold
7. coast
8. odd
9. locate
10. slope
11. throat
12. host
13. online
14. shock
15. solve
16. known
17. remote
18. stock
19. boast
20. globe

Challenge
bonus
approach
motion
continent
accomplish

Name _____ Date _____

Proofreading for Spelling

Find the misspelled words and circle them. Write them correctly on the lines below.

People were in shok when they heard the news that Tim was involved in the disappearance of the ancient weaving from the local museum. Tim seemed like a nice enough feloe who was knowne and recognized by several of the volunteers at the gift shop. He wroat a silly note to enclose with the toy blok kit he bought for his nephew. He also tried to loccate a gloab for his niece, but there were none in stoc.

Tim did boaste about planning a trip to the coest of South America but said he had to postpone it because of a sore throte. Then he asked about the weavers' video shon during the day. Needless to say, the museum staff was surprised when the security video showed Tim taking the ancient weaving and then covering up with it while he took a nap in the back!

Spelling Words
1. block
2. shown
3. oatmeal
4. wrote
5. fellow
6. scold
7. coast
8. odd
9. locate
10. slope
11. throat
12. host
13. online
14. shock
15. solve
16. known
17. remote
18. stock
19. boast
20. globe
Challenge
bonus
approach
motion
continent
accomplish

1. _____   7. _____

2. _____   8. _____

3. _____   9. _____

4. _____   10. _____

5. _____   11. _____

6. _____   12. _____

Sentence Fragments

A sentence must have a subject and a predicate to tell a complete thought. A **sentence fragment** is missing a subject, a predicate, or sometimes both.

fragment
Helped raise money for the soccer team.

Thinking Questions
Does this group of words have a subject that tells whom or what this sentence is about? Does it have a predicate that tells what happens or says something about the subject?

1–4. Write *sentence* if the group of words is a sentence. Write *fragment* if the group of words is not a sentence.

1. We made money for our team. _____

2. Held a fun fair for little kids. _____

3. Everyone on the team participated. _____

4. Activities all over the soccer field. _____

5–8. Write *subject* if the fragment is missing the part of the sentence that tells *whom* or *what*. Write *predicate* if the fragment is missing the part of the sentence that tells *what happens* or *what is*.

5. Tossed beanbags into a cardboard clown's mouth
_____

6. A team member with a polar bear outfit
_____

7. Posed for pictures with the bear _____

8. Kids with clown makeup _____

Name _____ Date _____

Run-on Sentences

A **run-on sentence** has two complete thoughts that run together. To correct a run-on sentence, write each complete thought as a separate sentence or form them into a compound sentence.

run-on sentence: They all worked together the project was a success.

separate sentences: They all worked together. The project was a success.

compound sentence: They all worked together, and the project was a success.

Thinking Questions
How many complete thoughts are in the sentence? Is there proper punctuation and capitalization or a conjunction?

Write *run-on* if the sentence is a run-on sentence. Write *correct* if the sentence is not a run-on sentence. For each run-on sentence, draw a line between the two complete thoughts.

1. We wanted to raise money, our class needed a new computer.

_____

2. Some people suggested a bake sale some wanted an arts-and-crafts fair.

_____

3. The class decided on an arts-and-crafts sale.

_____

4. One group made picture frames, another made baskets.

_____

5. Some parents helped also they made candleholders.

_____

6. We sold our arts and crafts to parents and students in other grades.

_____

Name _____ Date _____

Writing Complete Sentences

To change a sentence fragment to a complete
sentence, first identify what information is missing.
Then write a new sentence.

fragment	Worked together on a project.
complete sentence	Our school worked together on a project.
run-on	We raised money everyone had fun.
complete sentences	We raised money. Everyone had fun.

Thinking Questions
*What information is
missing from a fragment?
How can I fix a run-on?*

1–3.   **Change each fragment to a complete sentence.**

1. Made money for a new playground.

_____

2. Supported the kids in their community.

_____

3. Each class in school.

_____

4–6.   **Rewrite each sentence correctly.**

4. We had a fair we sold food from many countries.

_____

5. One booth sold tacos, another sold pizza.

_____

6. It was a success, we'll do it again next year.

_____

Writing Titles

When you write a title, capitalize

- the first word in the title.
- all important words in the title.
- a person's title, such as *Ms.* or *Dr.*

Do not capitalize *a*, *an*, or *the* unless it is the first word in the title.

1–4. **Write each title correctly in the space below.**

1. "the power of a community"

_____

2. the dallas morning news

_____

3. guide to volunteering

_____

4. "how p.o.w.w.o.w. saved a program"

_____

5–6. **Write each sentence correctly in the space below.**

5. The library has a copy of my favorite magazine, community service.

_____

6. Doug read a great article on fundraising called "the basics of building support."

_____

Name _____ Date _____

Sentence Fluency

> When you edit your writing, make sure to correct all sentence fragments and run-on sentences. Many experienced writers make their writing flow smoothly by varying the length of their sentences.
>
> For variety, combine two short, related sentences by inserting a comma and a conjunction between them. The words *and*, *but*, and *so* are conjunctions.
>
> Dora got on her bike. She rode down the street.
>
> Dora got on her bike, **and** she rode down the street.

1–5. Combine each pair of sentences using a comma and a conjunction. Use *and*, *but*, or *so*.

1. We belong to the service club at school. We find ways to help people.

   _____

2. Olivia was sick today. We took the homework assignment to her after school.

   _____

3. Every year, our class does a project to help the community. This year will not be different.

   _____

   _____

4. Gary called his friends to help. They were at football practice.

   _____

5. Dad cooks dinner every night. Bridget watches her little sister.

   _____

Focus Trait: Ideas
Why Events and Actions Happen

Good writers show or hint at why events happen and why
characters act the way they do. The plot helps direct the actions
of the characters. A plot has a beginning, middle, and end.

Plot Event or Action	Reason Why
The Words on Wheels program is in its last week.	The library has no more money to pay for gas or buy books.

Read each event or action from "The Power of W.O.W.!" Then
give the reason why it happened.

Plot Event or Action	Reason Why
1. Ileana, Shane, and Jason decide to have a car wash.	
2. Ileana does not accept a donation from her uncle, Mr. Diaz.	
3. A television news van comes to the car wash.	
4. The car wash becomes busier, and the kids begin making more money.	

Reader's Guide

Stormalong

Post Cards to Home

Stormalong writes post cards to a friend back home in Cape Cod about his adventures. Use details from the story to complete Stormalong's post cards home.

Read pages 144–145. Stormalong impresses the crew of the *Lady of the Sea* by fighting a giant octopus. In Stormalong's post card, include details from the story that reflect his point of view.

Hello!
I fought an octopus today.
_____
_____
_____
_____

Stormalong

Next, read page 147. Now Stormalong is writing about his move to Kansas. As Stormalong, write in first person to explain why you are moving.

Hello!
_____
_____
_____
_____
_____
_____
_____

Stormalong

Finally, read about Stormalong's trouble on the English Channel on pages 149–151. What happened? How does Stormalong feel about it? Write another post card.

Stormalong

Think about the end of the story. What can you infer about how Stormalong feels? Explain how he feels and tell why.
Use your own words.

_____

_____

_____

_____

_____

_____

Reference Materials

> **dispose**, *v.* to throw away
> **harbor**, *n.* a sheltered body of water where ships can anchor safely
> **mineral**, *n.* a natural substance, such as diamonds or coal, that is not plant or animal
> **mine**, *v.* to dig a tunnel or hole in order to find minerals
> **valuable**, *adj.* worth a lot of money

1–4. **Choose a word from the sample dictionary entries above to complete each sentence.**

1. When silver was discovered in Colorado, thousands of

   people went west to _____ for it and get rich.

2. Like gold, silver is rare, so even a little bit is _____ .

3. If the silver is buried deep, miners must move a lot of

   earth and _____ of it safely.

4. Silver is just one important _____ . Others

   include coal, iron, and copper.

5–7. **Use the given word in a sentence. Use a dictionary to confirm word meanings.**

5. errand

   _____

6. popular

   _____

7. trampled

   _____

Homophones

Basic 1–10. Write the Basic Word that best completes each sentence.

Spelling Words

1. I cannot _____ for my grandmother's birthday party.

2. We are going to celebrate in two _____ with a picnic.

3. I hope that my sprained ankle will _____ by then.

4. Organizing the party has been a real _____.

5. People have _____ gifts from all over the country.

6. I _____ that my uncle is buying a piñata.

7. I asked my grandmother not to _____ at the presents in the closet.

8. I bought Grandmother a spinning weather _____.

9. She can put it on the _____ of the roof.

10. Most of the guests will be adults. I will be the only _____.

1. wait
2. weight
3. heard
4. herd
5. days
6. daze
7. heel
8. heal
9. peak
10. peek
11. sent
12. cent
13. scent
14. feet
15. feat
16. vain
17. vane
18. vein
19. miner
20. minor

Challenge
raise
raze
rays
principal
principle

Challenge 11–14. Write a short article for your school about holding a book sale to help get money for new school playground equipment. Use four Challenge Words. Write on a separate sheet of paper.

Name _____ Date _____

Spelling Word Sort

Write each Basic Word beside the correct heading.

/ā/ sound	Basic Words: Challenge Words: Possible Selection Words:
/ĕ/ sound	Basic Words:
/ē/ sound	Basic Words: Possible Selection Words:
/ī/ sound	Basic Words:
Other homophones	Basic Words: Challenge Words: Possible Selection Words:

Challenge Add the Challenge Words to your Word Sort.

Connect to Reading Look through "Stormalong." Find words that sound alike but have different spellings and meanings. Add them to your Word Sort.

Spelling Words

1. wait
2. weight
3. heard
4. herd
5. days
6. daze
7. heel
8. heal
9. peak
10. peek
11. sent
12. cent
13. scent
14. feet
15. feat
16. vain
17. vane
18. vein
19. miner
20. minor

Challenge
raise
raze
rays
principal
principle

Proofreading for Spelling

Find the misspelled words and circle them. Write them correctly on the lines below.

To swim with manatees, you need a guide and snorkeling gear, including fins for your feete that fit your hele comfortably. You might feel like a minar in all of the gear, but it is all necessary. Sometimes your search for manatees is in vian and all you experience is the secnt of the sea, but often you can get a piek at the giant mammals moving slowly through the water if you wate long enough. You'll find you can stop on a cint when you see a manatee, and you can be so excited you'll feel like a vien might pop. Swimming with a hurd of manatees can put you in a daiz. A manatee's wieght can reach 3,000 pounds, and it can grow to be 13 feet long. If you ever get to swim with these gentle giants, you will be very lucky!

1. _____
2. _____
3. _____
4. _____
5. _____
6. _____
7. _____
8. _____
9. _____
10. _____
11. _____
12. _____

Spelling Words

1. wait
2. weight
3. heard
4. herd
5. days
6. daze
7. heel
8. heal
9. peak
10. peek
11. sent
12. cent
13. scent
14. feet
15. feat
16. vain
17. vane
18. vein
19. miner
20. minor

Challenge
raise
raze
rays
principal
principle

Capitalizing Historical Events and Documents

Proper nouns are always capitalized. Proper nouns are words that name a particular person, place, or thing. The names of important historical events and documents are also proper nouns and should be capitalized.

Thinking Question
What words name a particular event or document?

a war the American Revolutionary War
a document the Declaration of Independence

Remember, do not capitalize small words like *and*, *of*, and *the*.

Write these sentences correctly. Add capital letters when they are needed.

1. After the war of 1812, many pioneers went west.

_____

_____

2. Clipper ships were used in the california gold rush.

_____

_____

3. Clipper ships were not common after the civil war.

_____

_____

4. Lincoln signed the emancipation proclamation during the war.

_____

_____

Stormalong
Grammar: Proper Nouns

Capitalizing Titles

The titles of books, stories, and essays are **proper nouns** and should always be capitalized. Do not capitalize small words, such as *and*, *of*, and *the*, unless they begin the title.

book   *Treasure Island*
story   "Old Stormalong and the Octopus"

Remember, put the titles of book chapters, stories, and essays inside quotation marks.

Thinking Question
Which words are part of a title?

Write these sentences correctly. Add capital letters where they are needed. Be sure to underline book titles.

1. Is there a story about Stormalong in the book american tall tales?

_____

_____

2. The story "five fathoms tall" is about Stormy.

_____

_____

3. I wrote an essay for class called "why we like tall tales."

_____

_____

4. I loved the story "paul bunyan, the giant lumberjack."

_____

_____

Capitalizing Languages, People's Names, and Nationalities

The names of languages, people, and nationalities are **proper nouns.** They should always be capitalized.

languages	English, Spanish, Quechua, Arabic, Swahili
peoples' names	Alfred Bulltop Stormalong, Paul Bunyan
nationalities	Canadian, Spanish, Chilean, Saudi Arabian

Thinking Question
What words name a language, person, or nationality?

1–4. **Write these sentences correctly. Add capital letters where they are needed.**

1. Did sailors speak chinese when they sailed to Asia?

_____

_____

2. Do william and janet know why the Dover cliffs are white?

_____

_____

3. Stormy delivered cargo to italians and to indians.

_____

_____

4. The tall tale hero john henry is an american hero.

_____

_____

Writing Quotations

> Capitalize the first word of a quotation. If a quotation comes at the end of the sentence, place a comma and a space before the first quotation mark. Place end punctuation before the last quotation mark.
>
> The narrator said, "As he grew older, Stormy was the main attraction of Cape Cod."
>
> Stormy said, "The sea's my best friend."

1–6.   Write these sentences correctly. Add commas, capital letters, end marks, and quotation marks where they are needed.

1. The captain shouted hoist the anchor!

_____

2. Stormy said, A sailor's life is the only one for me.

_____

3. The book says, "the author uses exaggeration"

_____

4. A sailor asked "where will you settle down, Stormy"

_____

5. The first mate cried "we have to turn back"

_____

6. No one quite remembers how old Stormalong died the narrator said.

_____

_____

Word Choice

Less Exact Nouns	More Exact Nouns
The <u>boys</u> signed up for a tour of the <u>river</u>.	The <u>campers</u> signed up for a tour of <u>Rainbow River</u>.

1–8. Rewrite each sentence. Change the underlined words to exact nouns.

1. This summer, some <u>children</u> and I are going to sailing camp.

_____

2. We are looking forward to many exciting <u>things</u>.

_____

3. Sailing a boat through <u>water</u> is a real challenge.

_____

4. The early morning air can be chilly, so everyone wears warm <u>clothes</u>.

_____

5. From time to time, someone spots <u>animals</u> in the open water.

_____

6. One morning, <u>a boy</u> sees a dolphin and her calf swimming nearby.

_____

7. It takes a lot of <u>work</u> to sail a boat.

_____

8. At noontime, we catch a strong <u>wind</u> and speed toward shore.

_____

Focus Trait: Organization
Beginning a Story

A. **Identify the character and setting in the story opening. Then make a prediction about what the story problem might be.**

1. Sui Li crept down the stairs. She opened the cellar door and stepped in. She smelled dust and dampness. Her flashlight gave off light. The door shut behind her.

   Character: _____

   Setting: _____

   Story Problem: _____

B. **Read each story opening. Then write sentences to introduce a story problem.**

2. The waves slapped against the side of the sailboat, harder and harder. Tom's father said, "Look at how dark the sky is getting!"

   _____

   _____

   _____

3. The cave seemed miles wide. Amber stared in amazement at the strange rock formations.

   _____

   _____

   _____

4. James looked up and down the empty street. He called out into the silence, "Is anybody there?"

   _____

   _____

   _____

Invasion from Mars

PLAYBILL

A playbill is a program for a play. One of the things a playbill lists is a plot summary to entice viewers. Answer the questions below to help you create a plot summary for the playbill of *Invasion from Mars*.

Where and when does the story take place?

_____

By whom is the story told?

_____

List three major plot events.

- _____

- _____

- _____

When the aliens come out of the object, how does the crowd feel? Find the stage direction on page 183 that tells you this information.

_____

_____

How does the character Phillip's narration of the event help you understand the event?

_____

_____

Write a summary of the play for the playbill using the
information you gathered on the previous page. Make sure to
include the setting, main characters, and the main events, but don't
give away the most exciting parts! You want the audience to watch
the play to find out more.

INVASION FROM MARS
PLOT SUMMARY

_____

_____

_____

_____

_____

_____

_____

_____

_____

_____

_____

_____

_____

_____

PLAYBILL

INVASION FROM MARS

Suffixes *-y, -ous*

adventurous	handy	rocky
glorious	cloudy	chilly
scary	wondrous	glamorous

Complete each sentence with a word from above.

1. A pencil is a _____ thing to have when you are taking a test.

2. The _____ princess wore an expensive gown and jewels to the ball.

3. The _____ skier raced down a steep mountain.

4. The _____ sky made the air seem _____ .

5. The climb up the _____ cliff was difficult and tiring.

6. The _____ monster frightened the villagers.

7. At the end of the day, we watched a _____ sunset.

8. Their mouths dropped open at the _____ sight.

Invasion from Mars
Spelling: Vowel Sounds
/u/, /yoo/, and /oo/

Vowel Sounds /u/, /yoo/, and /oo/

Basic 1–11. Read the paragraph. Write the Basic Words that best complete the sentences.

The puppy running through the grocery store was the first

(1) _____ something was wrong. Diana stood

next to the (2) _____ and vegetable section. She

looked at a (3) _____ of bananas but chose an

orange instead. Suddenly, the (4) _____ dog

jumped into Diana's cart! It tore open a loaf of bread,

causing a (5) _____ to fly into Diana's face.

Startled, Diana squeezed the orange, and

(6) _____ exploded over Diana and a nearby man.

He was (7) _____ to Diana. He began to (8)

_____ with her. He said it was her fault that his

business (9) _____ was ruined! One worker had

to (10) _____ the dog. The cleaning

(11) _____ had to mop the floor.

Challenge 12–14. Write sentences that tell about jobs that people might have. Use three Challenge Words. Write on a separate sheet of paper.

Spelling Words

1. bunch
2. fruit
3. argue
4. crumb
5. crew
6. tune
7. juice
8. refuse
9. truth
10. young
11. clue
12. trunk
13. amuse
14. suit
15. rude
16. trust
17. dew
18. stuck
19. rescue
20. brush

Challenge
computer
mustard
tissue
customer
attitude

Spelling Word Sort

Invasion from Mars
Spelling: Vowel Sounds
/ŭ/, /yōō/, and /ōō/

Write each Basic Word beside the correct heading.

/ŭ/ spelled *u* followed by a consonant	Basic Words: Challenge Words: Possible Selection Words:
Other spellings for /ŭ/	Basic Words:
/yōō/ and /ōō/ spelled *u-consonant-e*	Basic Words: Challenge Words: Possible Selection Words:
/yōō/ and /ōō/ spelled *ue*	Basic Words: Challenge Words:
/yōō/ and /ōō/ spelled *ui*	Basic Words:
/ōō/ spelled *ew*	Basic Words: Possible Selection Words:
Other spellings for /yōō/ and /ōō/	Basic Words: Challenge Words:

Spelling Words

1. bunch
2. fruit
3. argue
4. crumb
5. crew
6. tune
7. juice
8. refuse
9. truth
10. young
11. clue
12. trunk
13. amuse
14. suit
15. rude
16. trust
17. dew
18. stuck
19. rescue
20. brush

Challenge
computer
mustard
tissue
customer
attitude

Challenge   Add the Challenge Words to your Word Sort.

Connect to Reading   Look through "Invasion from Mars." Find more words that have the /ŭ/, /yōō/, and /ōō/ spelling patterns on this page. Add them to your Word Sort.

Proofreading for Spelling

Find the misspelled words and circle them. Write them correctly on the lines below.

Sometimes trooth and fantasy are easily confused. That is what happened when a radio play, meant to amuise, created a panic. At that time, people were very in toon with stories of aliens from space. So, when a radio crue described a strange extraterrestrial crash, few people would argew that they didn't believe it.

According to the newsman, a bunsh of people were gathered beside the crash when suddenly an alien emerged. Old and yung alike were stuk to their seats as the story unfolded.

It was hours before people had a clew that the broadcast was a hoax. Frantic citizens called on authorities to rescew them. Finally, people settled down, but they grew skeptical. From then on, many would refuise to trest everything they heard on television or radio.

1. _____ 7. _____
2. _____ 8. _____
3. _____ 9. _____
4. _____ 10. _____
5. _____ 11. _____
6. _____ 12. _____

Spelling Words

1. bunch
2. fruit
3. argue
4. crumb
5. crew
6. tune
7. juice
8. refuse
9. truth
10. young
11. clue
12. trunk
13. amuse
14. suit
15. rude
16. trust
17. dew
18. stuck
19. rescue
20. brush

Challenge
computer
mustard
tissue
customer
attitude

Action Verbs

An **action verb** tells what a person or thing does.

action verb

A strange object <u>lands</u> near the school.
It <u>came</u> from the sky.

Thinking Question
Which words tell what a person or thing does?

1–10. Write the action verb in each sentence.

1. The object glows like the moon. _____

2. Students watch the object in shock. _____

3. A strange creature peers out a window.

_____

4. The event begins earlier in the day. _____

5. Many people hear a loud buzzing sound.

_____

6. A silver streak flashes overhead. _____

7. The object rises with a roar. _____

8. It disappears into the clouds. _____

9. The students stare at one another in amazement.

_____

10. Everyone returns to their work. _____

Main Verbs and Helping Verbs

Some verbs are more than one word. The **main verb** is the most important verb. The **helping verb** comes before the main verb.

helping verb   main verb
    Ryan is writing a science fiction story.

Thinking Questions
Which is the most important verb? Which verb comes before it?

1–10. Write *HV* above each helping verb. Write *MV* above each main verb.

1. Ryan has read much science fiction.

2. He was thinking about his favorite stories.

3. They have described distant galaxies.

4. Ryan is imagining a strange planet.

5. Ryan will write about the planet's creatures.

6. His characters are traveling to Earth.

7. They are dressed as humans.

8. They will visit New York City.

9. The extraterrestrials are living among us.

10. The story will frighten his friends.

Linking Verbs

A **linking verb** tells what someone or something is, or what someone or something is like. Most linking verbs are forms of the verb *be*.

linking verb
That story <u>is</u> scary.

Thinking Questions
Which word tells what a person or thing is? Which word tells what a person or thing is like?

1–8. **Underline the linking verb in each sentence.**

1. Science fiction was always my favorite type of story.

2. The stories are very imaginative.

3. In one story, a creature from Mars becomes lost on Earth.

4. The creature appears human.

5. A boy is kind to the creature.

6. Soon, the creature is comfortable at the boy's home.

7. The Martian becomes homesick on Earth.

8. That story seemed realistic in some ways.

Complete Sentences

A complete sentence expresses a complete thought. It contains a subject and a predicate. To change a sentence fragment to a complete sentence, identify what is missing. Then write a new sentence.

The movie characters.	The movie characters see a spaceship.

To correct a run-on sentence, write each complete thought as a separate sentence.

The spaceship appears out of the blue it lands in a field.	The spaceship appears out of the blue. It lands in a field.

1–3.   Change each fragment to a complete sentence.

1. Streaking across the sky.

_____

2. The pattern of the lights.

_____

2. Could be on a helicopter or an airplane.

_____

4–6.   Rewrite each run-on sentence correctly.

4. The lights at the top were red the lights around the bottom were yellow.

_____

5. The lights hovered over the park people started backing away.

_____

6. Then the strange lights disappeared the streetlights suddenly disappeared also.

_____

_____

Word Choice

Weak Verb	Strong Verb
Scientists made a spaceship for a flight to Venus.	Scientists designed a spaceship for a flight to Venus.

1–6. **Replace each underlined verb with a stronger verb. Write the new sentence on the line.**

1. Many astronauts thought about a trip to Venus.

_____

2. The rocket finally took off.

_____

3. It went through space at thousands of miles per hour.

_____

4. Its metal sides shone in the sunlight.

_____

5. The spaceship moved past the moon within hours.

_____

6. Soon the astronauts will walk on Venus.

_____

Focus Trait: Ideas
News Report

Make your writing strong by including specific, relevant facts, quotations, and other details to express your ideas.

Weak, General Ideas	Specific, Relevant Details
A comet came close to Earth recently. Some people feared it could hit Earth, but scientists said it came apart and won't be near Earth again for many years.	A comet passed within 22 million miles of Earth on October 16, 2011. "It broke apart," said Don Yeomans of NASA. The remains of the comet won't be near Earth again for 12,000 years.

Write a paragraph reporting on a fictional asteroid that approached Earth. Begin with the topic sentence shown below and include the most relevant and specific details from the list of ideas. Add a detail from your own knowledge or experience. Use precise language to state the facts.

Topic Sentence: An asteroid came near Earth on Tuesday.

_____

_____

_____

_____

Ideas

1. People called the asteroid 2427.
2. People said the asteroid was not a danger.
3. The asteroid came within 500,000 miles of Earth.
4. Some people worried about the asteroid.
5. An asteroid might have hit Earth and killed the dinosaurs.
6. "We can protect Earth from all asteroids," said a popular astronaut.

Name _____ Date _____

Lesson 7
READER'S NOTEBOOK

Coming Distractions:
Questioning Movies
Independent Reading

 Reader's Guide

Coming Distractions: Questioning Movies

Thumbs Up or Thumbs Down

Reread pages 204–208 of "Coming Distractions: Questioning Movies." Then answer the questions below.

List three opinions that the author states about movies.

1. _____

_____

2. _____

_____

3. _____

_____

List one fact that the author uses to support each opinion above.

1. _____

_____

2. _____

_____

3. _____

_____

Name _____ Date _____

Imagine you read the author's article online and want to send an e-mail to the author telling him what you think of it. Choose one opinion from your list. Do you think the author did a good job of supporting his opinions with facts? Tell the author what you think of his opinion. Make sure to support your opinion with reasons.

New Message
To: Frank W. Baker
From:
Subject: Your Article

_____

_____

_____

_____

_____

_____

_____

_____

_____

_____

_____

_____

_____

_____

Greek and Latin Word Parts *phon, photo, graph, auto, tele*

autograph   autobiography   automobile   symphony

photograph   telephone   photocopy   cinematographer

Read the words in the box above. Look for Greek and Latin word parts to help you understand the meaning of each word. Then use a word from the box to complete each sentence below.

1. The movie actress signed an _____ for her fan.

2. I used the _____ to call the theater for the movie schedule.

3. My mom drove the _____ to the movie theater.

4. At the movie premiere, I used a camera to take a _____ of the actors.

5. The movie director wrote an _____ about his life.

6. The _____ won an award for his filming technique.

7. The movie soundtrack features a _____ by a famous composer.

8. I will _____ this movie article from the library to share with the class tomorrow.

Name _____ Date _____

Lesson 7
READER'S NOTEBOOK

**Coming Distractions:
Questioning Movies**
Spelling: Vowel Sounds
/o͞o/ and /o͝o/

Vowel Sounds /o͞o/ and /o͝o/

Basic 1–10. Complete the puzzle by writing the Basic Word for each clue.

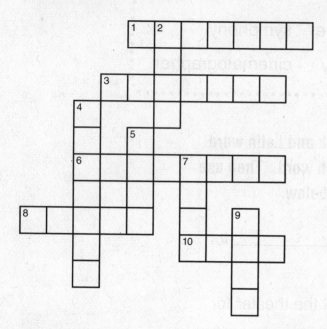

Across

1. bent or twisted
3. not sensible
6. a collection of recipes
8. a seat with legs but no arms
10. a bent object used to hold something

Down

2. the cover on a house
4. mammal with masklike face markings
5. thick hair from sheep
7. low, woody plant; a shrub
9. instrument used for work

Challenge 11–14. You've just finished your homework assignment. Before putting it in your backpack, you check it over for errors. Tell what you might find. Use four Challenge Words. Write on a separate sheet of paper.

Spelling Words

1. bloom
2. cookbook
3. tool
4. shampoo
5. put
6. wool
7. stool
8. proof
9. prove
10. group
11. brook
12. foolish
13. bush
14. crooked
15. booth
16. raccoon
17. hook
18. groom
19. roof
20. soup

Challenge
bulletin
cocoon
cushion
proofread
marooned

Spelling Word Sort

Coming Distractions:
Questioning Movies
Spelling: Vowel Sounds
/o͞o/ and /o͝o/

Write each Basic Word beside the correct heading.

/o͞o/ spelled *oo*	**Basic Words:** **Challenge Words:** **Possible Selection Words:**
Other spellings for /o͞o/	**Basic Words:**
/o͝o/ spelled *oo*	**Basic Words:** **Possible Selection Words:**
/o͝o/ spelled *u* followed by a consonant	**Basic Words:** **Challenge Words:**

Spelling Words

1. bloom
2. cookbook
3. tool
4. shampoo
5. put
6. wool
7. stool
8. proof
9. prove
10. group
11. brook
12. foolish
13. bush
14. crooked
15. booth
16. raccoon
17. hook
18. groom
19. roof
20. soup

Challenge
bulletin
cocoon
cushion
proofread
marooned

Challenge   Add the Challenge Words to your Word Sort.

Connect to Reading   Look through "Coming Distractions: Questioning Movies." Find words in the selection that have the /o͞o/ and /o͝o/ spelling patterns on this page. Add them to your Word Sort.

Proofreading for Spelling

**Coming Distractions:
Questioning Movies**
Spelling: Vowel Sounds
/o͞o/ and /o͝o/

**Find the misspelled words and circle them. Write them correctly
on the lines below.**

The next time you go to a movie, be sure to stay putt
until the end to watch the credits. Some people think it's
fullish, but the credits list the people involved in the movie.
They are also prouf of the work the groop did.

I now invite you to take a moment to picture some
of the following scenes that might be created on the set:
flowers in blewm, a family in a restaurant buth enjoying
bowls of hot sewp, a bottle of shampo on a rock by a brock,
and a veterinarian showing a young girl how to properly
groum her puppy. It takes many people to create these
simple scenes.

I recently visited a movie studio and went behind the
scenes. I met some of the people who make movie scenes
scary, exciting, or magical. I can proov it, too. I took a zillion
pictures!

1. _____	7. _____
2. _____	8. _____
3. _____	9. _____
4. _____	10. _____
5. _____	11. _____
6. _____	

Spelling Words

1. bloom
2. cookbook
3. tool
4. shampoo
5. put
6. wool
7. stool
8. proof
9. prove
10. group
11. brook
12. foolish
13. bush
14. crooked
15. booth
16. raccoon
17. hook
18. groom
19. roof
20. soup

Challenge
bulletin
cocoon
cushion
proofread
marooned

**Coming Distractions:
Questioning Movies**
Grammar: Verb Tenses

Past, Present, and Future Tenses

The **present tense** shows action happening now.

The **past tense** shows that an action already happened. Form the past tense by adding *-ed* to the end of a regular verb. If the verb ends in *e*, drop the *e* before adding *-ed*.

The **future tense** shows action that has not happened yet. The future tense is formed by using the helping verb *will* plus a verb.

present tense
I <u>watch</u> a movie with my family.

past tense
I <u>watched</u> a movie with my family.

future tense
I <u>will watch</u> a movie with my family.

Thinking Question
When does the action take place?

1–3. Write the verb given in parentheses in the past tense.

1. (walk) I _____ to the movie theater with my dad.

2. (amaze) The special effects in the movie _____ us!

3. (impresses) The actress _____ the critics with her moving performance.

4–5. Write the verb given in parentheses in the future tense.

4. (look) The new movie _____ great!

5. (walk) I _____ to the movie theater with my dad.

Helping Verbs and Past Participles

A **helping verb** such as *have, has,* or *had* comes before the main regular verb and tells more about what happened in the past. Helping verbs must agree with the subject of the sentence. Use these helping verbs with past participles.

The **past participle** of a regular verb is the the past-tense form: add *-ed* to the end of the regular verb. If the verb ends in *e*, drop the *e* before adding *-ed*. Past participle forms use helping verbs show past action.

They <u>have watched</u> that movie three times.

She <u>has liked</u> the movie as well.

Thinking Questions
Does the main verb end with -ed? Is it used with a helping verb?

Write the past participle of the verb in parentheses. Underline the helping verb.

1. Jane's aunt has (perform) _____ stunts for movies.

2. She has (work) _____ on a movie about spies.

3. Many action movies have (include) _____ amazing stunts.

4. Jane's aunt had (learn) _____ how to do stunts safely.

Underline the past participle in each sentence. Write the appropriate helping verb.

5. I _____ enjoyed many comedy movies.

6. That director _____ filmed some of the funniest comedies.

7. We _____ waited to see that actor's latest movie.

8. He _____ appeared on the movie screen many times.

Consistent Use of Tenses

Choose a verb tense to write in and continue to write in that tense. When you write about a particular time in a paragraph or sentence, all of the verbs should be in the same tense.

past tense: I <u>watched</u> a movie with a friend. After the movie, we <u>discussed</u> it.

present tense: We still <u>remember</u> and <u>laugh</u> at the funny parts.

future tense: Next time, we <u>will watch</u> a scary movie.

> **Thinking Question**
> *Are the verbs telling about a particular time all in the same tense?*

1–5. Choose the correct verb tense for the sentences. Write the correct verb on the line.

1. (go/will go) Tomorrow I will see a movie with my family.

   Then we _____ out to dinner.

2. (will like/liked) The scenery amazed me! I especially

   _____ the scene at the beach.

3. (admire, admired) We chose the movie because my mom

   has _____ its star for a long time.

4. (will buy/buy) First, we will buy movie tickets, and then we

   _____ some popcorn and drinks.

5. (liked/like) I love movies about cats! I also

   _____ movies about dogs.

Name _____ Date _____

Lesson 7
READER'S NOTEBOOK

Coming Distractions:
Questioning Movies
Grammar: Spiral Review

Fragments and Run-On Sentences

A sentence **fragment** is missing a subject, a predicate, or sometimes both. To correct a fragment, identify what is missing. Then write a new sentence with the missing part.

fragment: Has produced some amazing movies.

complete sentence: That studio has produced some amazing movies.

A **run-on sentence** has two complete thoughts that run together. To correct a run-on sentence, write each complete thought as a separate sentence.

run-on sentence: I will see the movie soon animated movies are my favorites.

correct sentences: I will see the movie soon. Animated movies are my favorites.

Write *correct* if the group of words is a correctly written sentence. Write *fragment* if the group of words is a fragment. Write *run-on* if the group of words is a run-on sentence. Change each fragment to a complete sentence. Rewrite each run-on sentence correctly.

1. An animated movie about a baby penguin.

   _____

2. Everyone will enjoy that character he is cute and funny.

   _____

3. Many animated movies have featured animal characters.

   _____

Sentence Fluency

When you write about a particular time in a sentence or paragraph, make sure the verbs are all in the same tense. Change the tense only to show a change in time.

Mixed Tenses	Same Tense
My cousin Susan takes acting lessons. She will want to be an actress.	My cousin Susan takes acting lessons. She wants to be an actress.

Rewrite each pair of sentences by changing the underlined verbs to the tense shown in parentheses.

1. Last year, Susan got a small role in a comedy. She will play a waitress. (past)

   _____

   _____

2. My entire family will go to opening night. We clapped loudly at the end! (past)

   _____

   _____

3. Now I own the DVD. I kept it on my bookshelf. (present)

   _____

4. Maybe someday I will act in the movies. Maybe I design costumes. (future)

   _____

   _____

Focus Trait: Word Choice
Using Precise Language

Read each sentence. Then rewrite the sentence using more
precise language and concrete details.

Poor Word Choice	Precise Word Choice
1. Everybody doesn't like movies where a lot of things happen fast.	
2. Most newspapers provide articles that tell whether a movie is good or bad.	
3. Different sounds in movies make them better.	
4. The clothes that actors wear are an important part of a movie.	
5. A good movie advertisement makes you want to see the movie.	

Reader's Guide

Me and Uncle Romie

Drawing the Bridge

When James arrives in New York, he feels very far from home. Answer the questions below to draw a picture of what James learns about people who live in different places.

Read pages 232–234. How are Harlem and North Carolina the same? How are they different? List the similarities and differences James lists as he spends his first day in New York.

_____

_____

_____

_____

_____

Read page 238. What does Uncle Romie say about people who live in different places?

_____

_____

_____

Which details on page 239 help you confirm that this is true?

_____

_____

_____

_____

Name _____ Date _____

What has James learned about people who live in places
different from his home? Imagine that you are James
writing in his journal about his experiences. Draw a picture
and write what you have learned.

Name _____ Date _____

Figurative Language

chow down   head over heels   good as gold

heart of gold   feast or famine   safe and sound

Rewrite each sentence using one of the idioms above.

1. My mother helps others because she is so kind and loving.

   _____

2. The quiet children were very well behaved during the long car trip.

   _____

   _____

3. When I finally sat down for lunch, I ate quickly without talking.

   _____

   _____

4. My best friend really loves the movie we watched.

   _____

5. The mother couldn't rest until all her children were tucked in their beds at home.

   _____

   _____

6. When I go to the library, I either see many books I want to read or none at all. It's always too many or too few.

   _____

   _____

Vowel Sounds /ou/, /ô/

Basic 1–10. Read the paragraph. Write the Basic Words that best complete the sentences.

I am a (1) _____ member of my school's bird-watching club. Every Saturday we leave at (2) _____ to go to the national park. Today, we looked for a (3) _____. It was sunny at first, but then it got (4) _____. Our adviser reminded us not to speak (5) _____ as we scanned the skies. Megan thought she saw something, but it was a (6) _____ alarm. Then we saw a bird fly from the (7) _____. We watched it (8) _____ a field mouse. The bird spread its wings wide, and it seemed to (9) _____ in the air. Suddenly, the bird dived and grabbed its meal with a sharp (10) _____!

Challenge 11–14. Write an e-mail message to your friend telling about a sporting event you have seen. Use four Challenge Words. Write on a separate sheet of paper.

Spelling Words

1. aloud
2. bald
3. hawk
4. south
5. faucet
6. proud
7. claw
8. tower
9. stalk
10. couple
11. howl
12. false
13. dawn
14. allow
15. drown
16. pause
17. fault
18. cause
19. amount
20. cloudier

Challenge
applaud
foul
browse
gnaw
doubt

Name _____ Date _____

Spelling Word Sort

Me and Uncle Romie
Spelling:
Vowel Sounds /ou/, /ô/

Write each Basic Word beside the correct heading.

/ou/ spelled *ou*	Basic Words: Challenge Words: Possible Selection Words:	
/ou/ spelled *ow*	Basic Words: Challenge Words: Possible Selection Words:	
Other sounds for *ou*	Basic Words:	
/ô/ spelled *aw*	Basic Words: Challenge Words:	
/ô/ spelled *au*	Basic Words: Challenge Words: Possible Selection Words:	
/ô/ spelled *a* before *l*	Basic Words: Possible Selection Words:	

Spelling Words

1. aloud
2. bald
3. hawk
4. south
5. faucet
6. proud
7. claw
8. tower
9. stalk
10. couple
11. howl
12. false
13. dawn
14. allow
15. drown
16. pause
17. fault
18. cause
19. amount
20. cloudier

Challenge
applaud
foul
browse
gnaw
doubt

Challenge Add the Challenge Words to your Word Sort.

Connect to Reading Look through "Me and Uncle Romie." Find more words that have the /ou/ and /ô/ spelling patterns on this page. Add them to your Word Sort.

Name _____ Date _____

Proofreading for Spelling

Find the misspelled words and circle them. Write them correctly on the lines below.

Mr. Rico's students are planning to paint a mural on the wall outside their classroom. Mr. Rico turns on the fawcet and rinses the brushes off. He checks the amont of paint available for the project while the students think alowd.

Everyone has a different idea. Rosa wants to paint a cuple of bawld eagles sitting high up on a towor. Jason thinks the mural should show a coyote letting out a houl at the silvery moon. Aidan says he wants to paint a box of matches with the words "Do Not Play With Matches." Matches are the cauze of many fires due to human falt. And Victoria wants to know if Mr. Rico will alow her to paint a race car. Mr. Rico likes everyone's ideas.

Before the students get started, Mr. Rico says, "Don't droun your brush with too much paint."

1. _____   7. _____
2. _____   8. _____
3. _____   9. _____
4. _____   10. _____
5. _____   11. _____
6. _____

Spelling Words

1. aloud
2. bald
3. hawk
4. south
5. faucet
6. proud
7. claw
8. tower
9. stalk
10. couple
11. howl
12. false
13. dawn
14. allow
15. drown
16. pause
17. fault
18. cause
19. amount
20. cloudier

Challenge
applaud
foul
browse
gnaw
doubt

Present Progressive Tense

Progressive forms of verbs show action that continues over time. To make the progressive form of a verb, add *-ing* to the main verb. Use a form of *be* as a helping verb.

The **present progressive tense** describes something that is continuing to happen now. It uses the verb *is*, *am*, or *are* as a helping verb.

He <u>is</u> <u>playing</u>.

Thinking Questions
Is the action taking place over a period of time? Is it happening in the present?

1–7. Write the words that form the present progressive tense in each sentence.

1. The kids are kicking a ball in the street.

_____

2. I am enjoying my game with the neighbors.

_____

3. The boys and girls are forming two teams.

_____

4. The ball is bouncing over the curb.

_____

5. The city street is getting noisier and livelier.

_____

6. I am remembering the quiet streets in my hometown.

_____

7. The sky is becoming darker by the minute.

_____

Past Progressive Tense

The **past progressive verb tense** describes something that continued in the past. It uses the verb *was* or *were* as a helping verb.

He <u>was</u> <u>working</u>.

Thinking Questions
Is the action taking place over a period of time? Is it happening in the past?

1–12.   Underline the words that form the past progressive verb in each sentence.

1. The artist was making amazing pictures in his studio.

2. An art gallery was showing them last month.

3. Everyone was admiring his art.

4. We were working together on some collages.

5. The pictures were hanging on the walls of the studio.

6. They were creating collages last year at school.

7. I was using photographs for my collages last year.

8. My friends were collecting photos of animals for me.

9. Also, I was cutting out comic strips for another collage.

10. I was showing that collage at my school's art show last winter.

11. I was telling my friends about my plans for the next collage.

12. They said they were wondering what I would do next.

Present, Past, and Future Progressive

Use progressive forms of verbs to show action that continues over time.

To make the progressive form of a verb, add *-ing* to the present-tense form of the main verb. Use a form of *be* as a helping verb.

For future progressive, use *will be* as the helping verb.

Thinking Questions
Is the action taking place over a period of time? Is it happening in the present, past, or future?

present progressive	I <u>am learning</u> about the city.
past progressive	I <u>was missing</u> my family.
future progressive	I <u>will be remembering</u> my visit.

1–4. **Write the sentences. Change each underlined verb into a progressive form. Use the progressive form identified in parentheses.**

1. I <u>visit</u> my cousins in Chicago. (present progressive)

_____

2. The streets <u>overflow</u> with traffic and people. (present progressive)

_____

3. The crowds <u>will stay</u> until late in the evening. (future progressive)

_____

4. I <u>planned</u> to go home on Sunday, but now I want to stay longer! (past progressive)

_____

Kinds of Sentences

Kind of Sentence	End Mark	Example
Statement	period (.)	Tomoko is waiting at the bus stop.
Question	question mark (?)	Does this bus go by the aquarium?
Command	period (.)	Get in line to buy a ticket.
Exclamation	exclamation mark (!)	That line is so long!

1–6. Write the correct end mark for each sentence. Then label each sentence *statement, question, command,* or *exclamation*.

1. The city streets are very busy _____

2. That bus is going so fast _____

3. Can you give me directions _____

4. Look both ways _____

5. I've never seen such a big crowd

_____

6. I am headed uptown _____

7–12. Correct six errors in this ad. There are two missing capital letters and four incorrect or missing end marks.

 Are you visiting our beautiful city soon! do you wonder how you'll ever find your way around town? Jonny's Guided Walking Tour is here to help. let one of our cheerful tour guides show you around, or use one of our easy-to-read maps? Either way, you'll learn about our city's rich history and see all of its important landmarks Everyone agrees. Jonny's Guided Walking Tours are totally cool

Ideas

> Help readers follow your ideas and the events you
> write about by using verb forms and verb tenses
> correctly.
>
> Use progressive verb forms for actions that happen
> over a period of time.
>
> Use the same verb tense for actions that happen at
> the same time.

**Read each pair of sentences. Choose the correct verb tense or form
for the second sentence. Write the correct verb form on the line.**

1. I plan to visit my cousin's house this summer. Now I

   _____ what I will want to do there. (listed/am

   listing)

2. My cousin lives on a farm out west. I _____

   in a big city in the east. (live, lived)

3. I was nervous about going. I _____ scared

   about being so far from home. (was getting, will get)

4. Then I talked to my cousin and his parents. I

   _____ how much fun we had when he came

   to visit me. (will be remembering, remembered)

5. Last time I visited him, we were three years old. We _____

   everywhere with the adults. (will go, went)

6. This time, we will be doing things by ourselves. I hope we

   _____ in his pond most of the time. (will be

   swimming, swam)

Focus Trait: Organization
Book Report

A. Read the book report sentences. Write the letters of the sentences in the correct order.

(A) I like this book because it compares two settings. (B) However, my favorite setting is the farm in North Carolina. (C) The book also has realistic characters. (D) The first setting is New York City. (E) My favorite character is the boy's uncle. (F) New York is crowded and exciting.

_____

B. Read the topic sentence below. Organize a complete paragraph that supports the topic with details.

Topic Sentence: The book I have read that has the most interesting setting

is _____ .

_____

_____

_____

_____

_____

Reader's Guide

Dear Mr. Winston

Mixed Messages

Reread page 262. Use details from Cara's letter to summarize what Cara writes to the librarian.

_____

_____

_____

Based on the letter, write in the thought ballon what Cara wants to tell her dad.

Dad,

What text evidence from the letter did you use to infer Cara's thoughts on page 262?

_____

_____

_____

Now turn to page 266 and respond to the items below.

Reread paragraphs 3, 4, and 5 of the letter on page 266. Use details
from Cara's letter to summarize what happened to the box.

_____

_____

_____

Based on the letter, write in the thought bubble what
Cara wants to tell her dad.

Dad,

What text evidence from the letter helped you make inferences about
Cara's thoughts on page 266?

_____

_____

_____

Antonyms

honest	thoughtful	borrow	healthy
genuine	ashamed	guilty	nearby

Read each sentence. Rewrite each using one of the antonyms above.

1. My wallet is made from fake leather.

   _____

2. I was proud when I threw the baseball through my

   neighbor's window.

   _____

   _____

3. We went shopping at a distant mall.

   _____

4. Monica asked if I could lend her my book.

   _____

5. My sister was sick.

   _____

6. I was lying when I said I liked to eat liver and onions.

   _____

7. She is a very thoughtless person.

   _____

8. My brother thinks that I am innocent of taking his

   baseball glove.

   _____

   _____

Dear Mr. Winston
Spelling:
Vowel + /r/ Sounds

Vowel + /r/ Sounds

Basic 1–10. Complete the puzzle by writing the Basic Word for each clue.

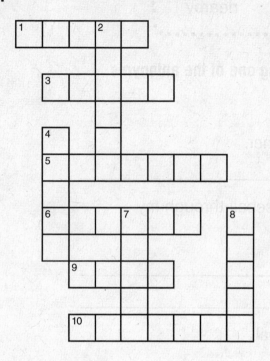

Across

1. unkind
3. a piece of cloth worn around neck or head
5. to make something ready
6. to mend
9. back
10. to discover differences and similarities

Down

2. not enough
4. a flash of light
7. a warning signal
8. to frighten

Challenge 11–14. You have watched a movie about taking a submarine trip deep in the ocean. Write a story about it. Use four Challenge Words. Write on a separate sheet of paper.

Spelling Words

1. spark
2. prepare
3. cheer
4. tear
5. scarf
6. scare
7. repair
8. earring
9. scarce
10. weird
11. sharp
12. rear
13. spare
14. gear
15. hairy
16. compare
17. alarm
18. harsh
19. upstairs
20. square

Challenge

weary
startle
appear
barnacle
awareness

Spelling Word Sort

Write each Basic Word beside the correct heading.

/îr/ spelled *ear*	Basic Words: Challenge Words:
/îr/ spelled *eer*	Basic Words:
Other spellings for /îr/	Basic Words:
/är/ spelled *ar*	Basic Words: Challenge Words: Possible Selection Words:
/âr/ spelled *are*	Basic Words: Challenge Words:
/âr/ spelled *air*	Basic Words:
Other spellings for /âr/	Basic Words: Possible Selection Words:

Spelling Words

1. spark
2. prepare
3. cheer
4. tear
5. scarf
6. scare
7. repair
8. earring
9. scarce
10. weird
11. sharp
12. rear
13. spare
14. gear
15. hairy
16. compare
17. alarm
18. harsh
19. upstairs
20. square

Challenge

weary
startle
appear
barnacle
awareness

Challenge Add the Challenge Words to your Word Sort.

Connect to Reading Look through "Dear Mr. Winston." Find words that have the vowel + /r/ spelling patterns in the chart. Add them to your Word Sort.

Proofreading for Spelling

Find the misspelled words and circle them. Write them correctly on the lines below.

I'm so jazzed! On our way to visit my grandparents, we saw a Grizzly Giant. You're probably thinking we saw a huge black, heiry bear with sharpp teeth, or that maybe we saw a very tall, weard person wearing a teer-shaped diamond earing. Nope. The Grizzly Giant is at least 200 feet tall and 30 feet around. It's a Sequoia tree!

Dad shifted into first geer, pulled over, and stopped the car. We went for a walk to look at these giant trees and discovered that you can even walk through some of them!

We heard clapping and a loud cher coming from the visitors center. Since we were on vacation and had lots of spar time, we decided to explore. Inside, the park ranger told us the upsteirs theater had a short movie about the park. She looked at her squar-shaped watch and said the next show started in five minutes.

Spelling Words

1. spark
2. prepare
3. cheer
4. tear
5. scarf
6. scare
7. repair
8. earring
9. scarce
10. weird
11. sharp
12. rear
13. spare
14. gear
15. hairy
16. compare
17. alarm
18. harsh
19. upstairs
20. square

Challenge

weary
startle
appear
barnacle
awareness

1. _____   6. _____

2. _____   7. _____

3. _____   8. _____

4. _____   9. _____

5. _____   10. _____

Dear Mr. Winston
Grammar: Compound and
Complex Sentences

Name _____ Date _____

Compound Sentences

A **compound sentence** has two simple sentences joined together. The separate sentences are joined by a comma (,) and a coordinating conjunction such as *and*, *or*, *but*, or *so*.

complete sentence   **complete sentence**
Some people read books, and others talked quietly.
          comma   **coordinating conjunction**

Thinking Questions
Is the sentence made up of two simple sentences? Is one word a coordinating conjunction with a comma before it?

1–8. Underline the simple sentences in each compound sentence. Circle the coordinating conjunction.

1. The girls went to the library, and they worked on their project.

2. They could do a report, or they could write a skit.

3. The library was quiet, but the girls were getting noisy.

4. Sophie made a joke, so everyone laughed.

5. Ms. Walker came over, and she put her finger to her lips.

6. The library is for everyone, but people should be considerate of others.

7. People must work quietly, or they will disturb others.

8. The girls could be quieter, or they could work at Sophie's house.

Name _____ Date _____

Complex Sentences

A **complex sentence** is made up of a simple sentence and a dependent clause, or a group of words that has a subject and a predicate. The two parts are joined by a subordinating conjunction such as *after, although, because, before, until, if, since,* and *while.*

The snake slithered under a rock   **simple sentence**
before the sun became too hot.   **dependent clause**

Thinking Question
Is the sentence made up of a simple sentence and a dependent clause with a subordinating conjunction?

1–4.   Read each complex sentence. Underline the simple sentence once. Underline the dependent clause twice. Circle the subordinating conjunction that joins the two.

1. Although Rodney loved most animals, he didn't like snakes.

2. Snakes startled him because they moved so quickly.

3. He ran away from a snake in the grass though he knew it wasn't poisonous.

4. He learned more about the snake after he saw it.

5–8.   Write a complete sentence by adding a simple sentence to the dependent clause. Put a comma between the two parts of the complex sentence.

5. Because that snake is poisonous

   _____

6. Although this snake is large

   _____

7. While you are at the zoo

   _____

8. After you look at the snake exhibit

   _____

Name _____ Date _____

Commas in Compound Sentences

Dear Mr. Winston
Grammar: Compound and Complex Sentences

A **compound sentence** has two or more complete thoughts joined together. Use a comma after each complete thought. Always put the comma before the coordinating conjunction.

Jane has a mouse, Mike has a snake, and I have a dog.

Thinking Question
Where is the coordinating conjunction?

1–6. Write each sentence. Put in commas where necessary.

1. I'm sorry my dog, Chipper, went into your yard and he will not do it again.

_____

_____

2. Chipper likes flowers so he wanted to smell your roses.

_____

_____

3. He crushed some plants but he didn't do it on purpose.

_____

_____

4. He jumped over the violets but he stepped on the daisies.

_____

_____

5. I looked over the fence I saw Chipper and I called him.

_____

_____

6. I could plant some more flowers or I could weed your garden for you.

_____

_____

Kinds of Nouns

Common Nouns	Proper Nouns	Singular Nouns	Plural Nouns
girl	Ann	apple	apples
city	Orlando	day	days
day	Thanksgiving	class	classes
month	June	fox	foxes

1–3. **Write each noun and tell whether it is *common* or *proper*.**

1. Joe and Sal each sneaked a box into their classroom.

_____

_____

2. Several holes had been poked into each lid with a pencil.

_____

_____

3. That morning, Ms. Li heard a strange noise under her desk.

_____

_____

4–6. **Write the plural form of the noun in parentheses.**

4. (sandwich) The children were eating their _____.

5. (box) Then, the lids popped off the two _____.

6. (frog) Suddenly, _____ were jumping all over the room.

Conventions

A **compound sentence** has two or more complete thoughts joined together. The separate ideas can be joined with a comma (,) and a conjunction such as *and*, *or*, *but*, or *so*.

Use a comma after each complete thought. Always put the comma before the conjunction.

Minnie is Alicia's dog. Alicia takes her everywhere.
Minnie is Alicia's dog, and Alicia takes her everywhere.

1–6. Combine the simple sentences into one compound sentence. Use a conjunction to join the two sentences. Use commas correctly.

1. The ice cream shop was empty. Alicia went in.

_____

2. She put her bag on the counter. She looked at the menu.

_____

3. The bag moved. A tiny dog peeked out.

_____

4. The lady behind the counter smiled. She spoke seriously.

_____

5. You can't bring pets here. You can bring service animals.

_____

6. You can leave the dog outside. You can come back later.

_____

Focus Trait: Organization
Opinions, Reasons, and Details

Good writers support their ideas with details and reasons.
When you explain your thoughts in an essay, group related ideas
together so they make sense to readers. Include only related
ideas.

The organization of your essay will depend on your topic.
For example, if you are explaining a process, describe the process
in the proper order.

Main Idea	Cara in "Dear Mr. Winston" is a likeable character.
Unrelated Detail	Mr. Winston knew Cara for several years.
Relevant Detail	She makes an honest mistake when she accidentally tells him who sold her the snake.

Read each idea about "Dear Mr. Winston." Write two
related, relevant details to support each idea.

1. **Idea:** Cara truly wants to know more about her snake.

   Detail _____

   _____

   Detail _____

   _____

2. **Idea:** Cara's father is more upset than her mother is.

   Detail _____

   _____

   Detail _____

   _____

José! Born to Dance

José's Performance Was Like…

A simile is a type of figurative language that compares two things using *like* or *as*. Read page 296. List three similes the author uses to describe José's dancing.

_____

_____

_____

_____

_____

_____

_____

_____

_____

_____

Imagine you are reporter and have attended one of José Limón's performances. Using the similes you found on page 296, write a review of José's performance. A review tells what is good and bad about something. What might the reporter say about José's career?

José Limón's Debut

José Limón performed at the theater on Saturday night. His performance was …

_____

_____

_____

_____

_____

_____

_____

_____

_____

_____

_____

Name _____ Date _____

Shades of Meaning

Synonyms are words that have similar meanings. They do not mean exactly the same thing. Synonyms may give us different feelings about the subject. For example, if you call someone's actions **bold,** you are praising him or her. If you call the actions **reckless,** you are criticizing.

Circle the synonym that best fits the context for each sentence. On the line, write why you chose this word.

1. Janelle sang all the time, and her teacher praised her (good, lovely) voice.

   _____

2. She was so (determined, stubborn) to succeed that she practiced every day.

   _____

3. She moved to the big city and rented a (cramped, little) room.

   _____

4. The busy city streets were (exciting, terrifying).

   _____

5. She worked at a restaurant to support herself, but she knew her real (job, profession) would be in music.

   _____

6. Janelle was (happy, thrilled) when she got her first paid singing job.

   _____

More Vowel + /r/ Sounds

Basic 1–10. Write the Basic Word that best replaces the underlined word or words in each sentence.

1. My older sister Pam gets up <u>at the beginning of the day</u> to run cross-country. _____

2. Running is her favorite <u>competition</u>. _____

3. There are <u>a little more than a dozen</u> students on her team. _____

4. Their <u>updated</u> uniforms are red and gold. _____

5. The race <u>path</u> goes through the woods near the creek. _____

6. Pam's teammates fight hunger and <u>dryness</u> as they train. _____

7. They often get <u>grubby</u> as they run through mud and under tree branches. _____

8. Their shoes get old and <u>used up</u> very quickly. _____

9. Muscles get <u>painful</u> and ache from all the activity. _____

10. The good feeling running gives Pam is <u>well deserving of</u> the effort. _____

Challenge 11–14. A friend of yours is planning a trip to another country. Write a letter wishing your friend a good trip. Use four Challenge Words. Write on a separate sheet of paper.

Spelling Words

1. learn
2. dirty
3. worn
4. sore
5. thirst
6. burn
7. record
8. cure
9. board
10. course
11. worth
12. early
13. return
14. pure
15. world
16. search
17. worse
18. thirteen
19. sport
20. current

Challenge
curious
thorough
earnest
portion
foreign

Spelling Word Sort

Write each Basic Word beside the correct heading.

/ôr/ spelled *or*	Basic Words: Challenge Words: Possible Selection Words:
/ôr/ spelled *ore*	Basic Words: Possible Selection Words:
Other spellings for /ôr/	Basic Words: Possible Selection Words:
/ûr/ spelled *ir* or *ur*	Basic Words: Possible Selection Words:
/ûr/ spelled *ear* or *or*	Basic Words: Challenge Words:
/yŏŏr/ spelled *ure*	Basic Words:
Other spellings for /yŏŏr/	Challenge Words:

Spelling Words

1. learn
2. dirty
3. worn
4. sore
5. thirst
6. burn
7. record
8. cure
9. board
10. course
11. worth
12. early
13. return
14. pure
15. world
16. search
17. worse
18. thirteen
19. sport
20. current

Challenge

curious
thorough
earnest
portion
foreign

Challenge   Add the Challenge Words to your Word Sort.

Connect to Reading   Look through "José! Born to Dance."
Find more words that have the vowel + /r/ spelling patterns
on this page. Add them to your Word Sort.

Proofreading for Spelling

Find the misspelled words and circle them. Write them correctly on the lines below.

Doris Humphrey was born in 1895 in Oak Park, Illinois. It was pur joy for her as a young child to lirn new dance routines. At first, she was stiff like a bord. Doris soon opened her own dance studio. In 1928, Doris and Charles Weidman left to form their own group in New York. They would go on to rekord their choreographic works and produce some of the outstanding performers in the wurld.

Her career ended due to arthritis, for which there was no kure. Not being able to dance hurt Doris werse than her ailment itself. Dance would always bern in her like a fire. However, she did not retern to California in serch of other work. Instead, she became José's mentor and the artistic director of his dance company. Doris was one of the founders of American modern dance.

1. _____
2. _____
3. _____
4. _____
5. _____
6. _____
7. _____
8. _____
9. _____
10. _____

Spelling Words

1. learn
2. dirty
3. worn
4. sore
5. thirst
6. burn
7. record
8. cure
9. board
10. course
11. worth
12. early
13. return
14. pure
15. world
16. search
17. worse
18. thirteen
19. sport
20. current

Challenge
curious
thorough
earnest
portion
foreign

Subject and Object Pronouns

A **subject pronoun** is a pronoun that tells who or what does the action of a sentence. An **object pronoun** is a pronoun that tells who or what receives the action of the verb.

subject pronoun

<u>He</u> studied dance for many years.

object pronoun

Grandmother made breakfast for <u>him</u> every morning.

Thinking Questions
What pronoun tells who or what does the action of the sentence? What pronoun tells who or what receives the action of the verb?

1–4. **Underline the subject pronoun in each sentence.**

1. We watched José dance in the show.

2. I couldn't wait to see the performance.

3. Have you ever seen a dance recital?

4. He should dance in all of the shows.

5–8. **Write the pronoun in parentheses that can take the place of the underlined word or words.**

5. (him, you) The birds sang to <u>José</u> during breakfast. _____

6. (them, us) Mama drank hot chocolate with <u>José and Grandmother</u>. _____

7. (him, me) José said to Grandmother, "Please give <u>José</u> more!" _____

8. (you, us) "Can you save some for <u>Mama and me</u>?" Grandmother asked, with a smile. _____

Reflexive and Demonstrative Pronouns

Reflexive pronouns show that a subject is performing an action on itself. They may also call attention to an action. **Demonstrative pronouns** point out specific people, places, things, or ideas.	

Reflexive pronouns	Demonstrative pronouns
myself, yourself, himself, herself, itself, ourselves, yourselves, themselves In dance class I can watch **myself** in the mirror. Jeff and Maria moved the mats **themselves**.	this, that, these, those **This** is a new dance to learn. **These** are your fellow students. **That** is where we practice. **These** are the lockers we use.

1–4. **Write the correct reflexive pronoun on the line in the sentences below.**

1. (herself, himself) Henry injured _____ while practicing a dance routine.

2. (myself, ourselves) I made the dance costumes _____!

3. (yourself, itself) Help _____ to some juice after you've mastered the dance steps.

4. (ourselves, yourselves) We dressed _____ before the dance recital.

5–8. **Write the correct demonstrative pronoun on the line in the sentences below.**

5. It's Saturday! _____ is the day of our recital!

6. Find the gray chairs in the closet. _____ are the chairs to set up in rows.

7. See the circle on the stage floor? _____ is where you stand at first.

8. Take this box. _____ are the programs to hand out to the audience.

Pronoun-Antecedent Agreement

An **antecedent** is a word or phrase that a following word refers back to. Pronouns often have antecedents.

antecedent   **pronoun**
Musicals are popular, and (they) feature singing and dancing.

In the above sentence, musicals is the antecedent. The word they is the pronoun that is used instead of repeating the word musicals. The pronoun agrees with its antecedent in number.

1–4.   Write the correct pronoun to complete each sentence.

1. (she, he) Fred Astaire was a famous actor, and _____ was well-known for his dancing.
2. (They, You) Ginger Rogers danced with Fred Astaire. _____ moved gracefully together.
3. (They, He) Gene Kelly danced in many movies. _____ are worth watching!
4. (They, It) Gene Kelly and Leslie Caron danced in *An American in Paris*. _____ was a great movie.

5–8.   Circle the pronoun in each sentence. Underline the antecedent.

5. Shirley Temple was a child star, and she could tap dance, too.
6. Musicals are fun, but they can be long.
7. Dancers need to be careful when they perform.
8. When my sister and I took tap dance lessons, we wore special shoes.

Plural Nouns

Singular	Plural
one **valley**	several **valleys**
a **bunny**	some **bunnies**
this **tooth**	these **teeth**
one **moose**	both **moose**

1–6. Write the plural form of the noun in parentheses to complete each sentence.

1. (hobby) Ballroom dancing is one of my aunt's _____.

2. (country) This type of dance is performed in many _____.

3. (man) Women and _____ wear fancy costumes.

4. (foot) Dancers kick their _____ and glide across the floor.

5. (city) Some _____ host ballroom dancing contests.

6. (key) One of the _____ to winning is practice, practice, practice!

7–12. Correct six errors in this paragraph. There are six plural nouns written incorrectly. Use proofreading marks.

My brother takes dance lessons on Fridayes. There are girls and boyes in his class. Last week, my parents and I watched his dance recital with many other families. I sat in the front row with several childs I knew. Some dancers wore tap shoes on their foots. Other dancers acted out stories. In one dance, the performers were dressed as sheeps! After the show, we went to two partys for the dancers.

Sentence Fluency

You can combine sentences with pronouns and subordinating conjunctions.

Choppy Sentences	Combined Sentences
José and his family stayed in Nogales. José and his family waited for permission to enter the United States.	José and his family stayed in Nogales while they waited for permission to enter the United States.

1–4. Combine each pair of sentences. Replace the underlined subject with a pronoun. Use the subordinating conjunction in parentheses. Write the new sentence on the line.

1. Papa decided to leave Mexico. Papa was worried about the war. (because)

   _____

   _____

2. José drew such beautiful pictures of trains. Everyone thought José would become an artist. (since)

   _____

   _____

3. José studied for three years. José learned English. (before)

   _____

   _____

4. José felt lonely. José walked around on a cold day. (when)

   _____

   _____

Name _____ Date _____

Lesson 10
READER'S NOTEBOOK

Focus Trait: Word Choice

José! Born to Dance
Writing: Informative Writing

Using Precise Words

To write about a topic, use words that are specific to the topic. These key words give readers a precise idea of what you are explaining.

Topic: Pet food	
Too General	**Precise**
dog food, water, scraps	nutrients, water, proteins, carbohydrates, fats, vitamins, minerals, kibble

Rewrite each sentence. Replace the underlined general words with more precise words. Choose words that are specific to the topic shown in parentheses.

1. (cooking) I cooked some bread yesterday.

_____

2. (science) We did an activity in the room after school.

_____

3. (math) Cut the paper in two pieces, and then fold each piece into a different shape.

_____

4. (sports) Janet made a point when she kicked the ball into the net.

_____

5. (computers) Use the thing that rolls around to move the pointer on your monitor screen.

_____

Name _____ Date _____

Unit 2
READER'S NOTEBOOK

Discovering Mars
Segment 1
Independent Reading

 Reader's Guide

Discovering Mars

Mars Trading Card

Design a trading card about Mars to include in a deck of cards for the solar system. Using information on pages 7–9, draw a picture of Mars and fill in the blanks.

Solar System Trading Cards

MARS

Another name for Mars:

_____

Where the name came from:

_____

_____

_____

Name _____ Date _____

Unit 2
READER'S NOTEBOOK

Discovering Mars
Segment 1
Independent Reading

Now answer some Frequently Asked Questions (FAQs) about Mars for the back of your trading card. What are some fun facts about Mars? Reread pages 9–11 and answer the questions to complete your card.

Solar System Trading Cards

DID YOU KNOW?

- Why does Mars look different over time?

  _____

  _____

- What are the large white areas at the poles?

  _____

  _____

- Why did people think Martians existed?

  _____

  _____

  _____

  _____

  _____

Name _____ Date _____

Unit 2
READER'S NOTEBOOK

Discovering Mars
Segment 2
Independent Reading

Reader's Guide

Discovering Mars

Mars Makes News

Mars made news in 1938 when a radio program caused panic among listeners in New Jersey. Use the information from pages 12–14 to write a news article that tells what caused the panic and how people reacted.

• NEWS TODAY •

1938

PANIC IN NEW JERSEY!

New Jersey _____

_____

_____

_____

_____

_____

_____

_____

_____

_____

_____

Name _____ Date _____

Unit 2
READER'S NOTEBOOK

Discovering Mars
Segment 2
Independent Reading

The planet Mars has made news many times since its discovery. Write a news article telling about the discovery of its two moons in 1877. Read page 15 to find the important facts to include in your article. Then, use pages 16–17 to help you complete a diagram to accompany your article.

❧ NEWS OF THE DAY ❧
MOONS DISCOVERED
NEAR MARS!

1877

Washington D.C. _____

_____

_____

_____

_____

_____

_____

Name: _____ _____

Diameter: _____ _____

Distance from Mars: _____ _____

Label the moons. Then write a caption for the diagram that compares the moons.

_____

_____

_____

_____

_____

Name _____   Date _____

Unit 2
READER'S NOTEBOOK

Discovering Mars
Segment 3
Independent Reading

Reader's Guide

Discovering Mars

Mission: A Space Rover to Mars

Imagine you are an engineer at NASA sending a space rover to explore the surface of Mars. Use the information on pages 19–25 to fill in the web below with details about the surface of Mars.

How big is Mount Olympus?
_____
_____
_____

What is the weather like on Mars?
_____
_____
_____

How long is Valles Marineris?
_____
_____
_____

Surface of Mars

What is the Northern Hemisphere of Mars like?
_____
_____
_____

What is the Southern Hemisphere of Mars like?
_____
_____
_____

Name _____ Date _____

Unit 2
READER'S NOTEBOOK

Discovering Mars
Segment 3
Independent Reading

Write a memo to your fellow colleagues at NASA explaining what kinds of things they should think about when planning the space rover mission to Mars. What special conditions should the engineers consider? What will the space rover need to be able to do? In your memo, give your solutions to the challenges the space rover mission may have.

MEMO

TO: NASA Engineers

FROM: _____

SUBJECT: Planning the Rover Mission to Mars

In planning the space rover mission, we will need to consider _____

_____

_____

_____

_____

_____

_____

_____

_____

_____

_____

Name _____ Date _____

Unit 2
READER'S NOTEBOOK

Discovering Mars
Segment 4
Independent Reading

 Reader's Guide

Discovering Mars

NASA Discovery Mission Series

Help create a timeline of NASA's discovery missions to Mars.
Reread pages 28–29 about NASA's Mariner missions. For each
mission, write a caption that tells how close the Mariner got to
Mars and why the mission was a success. Fill in the year of the
mission on the lines. Then write a caption that summarizes
the progress of the missions.

Mariner 4
Year:
_____

_____
_____
_____

Mariner 6 & 7
Year:
_____

_____
_____
_____

Mariner 9
Year:
_____

_____
_____
_____

_____
_____

Name _____ Date _____

Reread pages 34–37 about NASA's Viking missions.
Draw a picture to show the two tasks the missions
had. Then write a caption for your illustrations.

Viking I ————
Landing Date:

_____

Viking II
Landing Date:

_____

_____

_____

Name _____ Date _____

Unit 2
READER'S NOTEBOOK

Discovering Mars
Segment 5
Independent Reading

Reader's Guide

Discovering Mars

Volunteer: Mission to Mars

Astronauts need to be able to do many things to handle a mission in space. NASA interviews people who are interested in becoming astronauts to find the best people for the job. What kinds of questions should NASA officials ask to find good astronauts for the job?

Reread page 42.
Write a question based on what the astronauts on the cargo ship do.

Question: _____

_____

_____

Write a question based on what the mission to Mars is about.

Question: _____

_____

_____

Reread pages 44–45.
Write a question based on what is required for the astronauts physically.

Question: _____

_____

_____

Name _____ Date _____

Unit 2
READER'S NOTEBOOK

Discovering Mars
Segment 5
Independent Reading

Now imagine you are applying for the astronaut job. Answer the questions that you wrote on the previous page. Give answers that show why you would be a good astronaut for this mission.

_____

Answer 1: _____

_____

_____

_____

Answer 2: _____

_____

_____

_____

_____

Answer 3: _____

_____

_____

_____

_____

Name _____ Date _____

Unit 2
READER'S NOTEBOOK

Discovering Mars
Segment 6
Independent Reading

 Reader's Guide

Discovering Mars

Illustrated Guide to Terraforming Mars

Imagine you are on a committee that has come up with a plan to terraform Mars. Reread the ideas presented on pages 50–53.

First, summarize your plan for readers. How is Mars different from Earth? Tell what your plan will do to make Mars more like Earth.

_____

_____

_____

_____

_____

Now draw a three-step illustrated guide to your plan
to terraform Mars. Include a caption for each step.

STEP 1:

_____

Name _____ Date _____

Unit 2
READER'S NOTEBOOK

Discovering Mars
Segment 6
Independent Reading

STEP 2:

STEP 3:

Name _____ Date _____

Lesson 11
READER'S NOTEBOOK

Hurricanes: Earth's
Mightiest Storms
Independent Reading

Reader's Guide

Hurricanes: Earth's Mightiest Storms

Caption the Diagram

Read the first two paragraphs on page 324 of "Hurricanes: Earth's Mightiest Storms." Why does drawing air into the low-pressure area cause it to spiral?

_____

_____

_____

Take a close look at the diagram. In which hemisphere is the storm in the diagram located? How do you know? Write a caption to explain the diagram to readers.

_____

_____

_____

How does the diagram help you understand what the winds in a hurricane are like? Write a caption that describes them.

_____

_____

_____

_____

Read page 325. What is the eye of the storm like?

_____

_____

Why would people caught in the eye of a storm think that the storm has ended?

_____

_____

_____

Write a caption that explains what is happening in the eye of the storm and why it happens.

_____

_____

_____

Explain how the diagram helps you to understand what the eye of the storm is like.

_____

_____

_____

Suffixes -ful, -less, -ness, -ment

:..:
.   cheer   use   assign   still   .
.   success   dark   entertain   .
:..:

To complete each sentence below, select a word from the box and add the suffix -ful, -less, -ness, or -ment. Read the completed sentence to be sure it makes sense.

1. I have trouble being _____ when I hear a
   hurricane is coming.

2. The sudden _____ of the air told us the storm
   was approaching.

3. As the storm hit, doors and windows seemed
   _____ against a raging wind.

4. The storm knocked out our electricity, so we used candles
   and flashlights in the _____.

5. After the storm, my _____ was to take care
   of my little brother while the adults checked the storm
   damage.

6. I was _____ at keeping him busy for a while,
   but then he got bored.

7. It's difficult to find _____ for a five-year-old
   when you can't go outside and you don't have electricity!

Name _____ Date _____

Lesson 11
READER'S NOTEBOOK

Hurricanes: Earth's
Mightiest Storms
Spelling: Compound Words

Compound Words

Basic 1–10. Write the Basic Word that best replaces the underlined word or words.

My parents asked me to (1) <u>look after</u> my little sister. We waved (2) <u>see you later</u> as they drove down the (3) <u>lane from our garage</u>. Then we headed for town to get Amelia a (4) <u>short trim</u>. She was tired of always pushing her hair off her (5) <u>part of the face above her eyes</u>. Suddenly, it was like (6) <u>a person we did not know</u> had turned the sky green. People were yelling to get inside because a tornado was (7) <u>in the area</u>. We took shelter in a store's basement with (8) <u>more than twenty</u> other people. Fortunately, the storeowner kept a (9) <u>small, battery-powered lamp</u> in the basement, so we weren't stranded in the dark. In the end, the tornado missed our town, and we were (10) <u>fine</u>. Amelia and I had quite an adventure!

1. _____   6. _____
2. _____   7. _____
3. _____   8. _____
4. _____   9. _____
5. _____   10. _____

Challenge 11–14. Write a journal entry about taking a school trip with your class. Use four Challenge Words. Write on a separate sheet of paper.

Spelling Words

1. somebody
2. fireplace
3. nearby
4. toothbrush
5. homesick
6. make-believe
7. anything
8. all right
9. goodbye
10. forehead
11. classmate
12. flashlight
13. haircut
14. twenty-two
15. driveway
16. alarm clock
17. baby-sit
18. airport
19. forever
20. mailbox

Challenge
field trip
absent-minded
life jacket
skyscraper
nevertheless

Spelling Word Sort

Write each Basic Word beside the correct heading.

One word	**Basic Words:** **Challenge Words:** **Possible Selection Words:**
With a hyphen	**Basic Words:** **Challenge Words:** **Possible Selection Words:**
Two separate words	**Basic Words:** **Challenge Words:** **Possible Selection Words:**

Spelling Words

1. somebody
2. fireplace
3. nearby
4. toothbrush
5. homesick
6. make-believe
7. anything
8. all right
9. goodbye
10. forehead
11. classmate
12. flashlight
13. haircut
14. twenty-two
15. driveway
16. alarm clock
17. baby-sit
18. airport
19. forever
20. mailbox

Challenge
field trip
absent-minded
life jacket
skyscraper
nevertheless

Challenge Add the Challenge Words to your Word Sort.

Connect to Reading Look through "Hurricanes: Earth's Mightiest Storms." Find compound words. Add them to your Word Sort.

Proofreading for Spelling

Find the misspelled words and circle them. Write them correctly on the lines below.

Becky and her family heard that a hurricane was neerby. The local air porte was already closed to prepare for the high winds. That night, Becky found her flashlite and set her allarm clock so she would wake up early. In the morning, she called her friends to make sure they didn't need annything.

The hurricane's power seemed make beleive. Their brick fireplayce shook. The family took shelter in the basement. After the hurricane passed, they checked the damage and found trees in the driv-way. The mail box was sticking out of Becky's bedroom window. Becky realized how lucky she was to be all rite. She waved good-by to her broken window and wiped her fourhead in relief.

1. _____
2. _____
3. _____
4. _____
5. _____
6. _____
7. _____
8. _____
9. _____
10. _____
11. _____
12. _____

Spelling Words

1. somebody
2. fireplace
3. nearby
4. toothbrush
5. homesick
6. make-believe
7. anything
8. all right
9. goodbye
10. forehead
11. classmate
12. flashlight
13. haircut
14. twenty-two
15. driveway
16. alarm clock
17. baby-sit
18. airport
19. forever
20. mailbox

Challenge
field trip
absent-minded
life jacket
skyscraper
nevertheless

To, *Too*, and *Two*

Do not confuse the words *to, too,* and *two*. They sound the same, but they have different spellings and meanings.

Thinking Question
Which word makes sense in the sentence?

to means "in the direction of"	I ran **to** the porch when the rain started.
too means "also" or "in addition"	I brought my bike up on the porch **too.**
two is a number	My **two** brothers came out to watch the rain.

Complete each sentence with *to, too,* or *two,* as appropriate.
Write the correct sentence on the line.

1. The forecast says we will get (to, too, two) inches of rain.

   _____

2. Lightning strikes are amazing, but they can be scary, (to, too, two).

   _____

3. A storm with lightning has thunder (to, too, two).

   _____

4. Between the (to, too, two), I prefer thunder with its deep rumbling sounds.

   _____

5. I had planned on going (to, too, two) my friend's house until the storm was over.

   _____

There, They're, and *Their*

Do not confuse the words *there, they're,* and *their.* They sound the same, but they have different spellings and meanings.

Thinking Question
Which word makes sense in the sentence?

There means "in that place."	We go **there** to watch storms roll in.
They're is a contraction of *they are.*	**They're** my cousins.
Their means "belonging to them."	I love to spend time at **their** house.

Complete each sentence with *there, they're,* or *their.* Write the correct sentence on the line.

1. My friends Joe and Julie told me (there, they're, their) neighborhood was hit by the tornado.

   _____

2. I went over (there, they're, their) to help clean up the damage.

   _____

3. (There, They're, Their) house is still standing, but the roof is gone.

   _____

4. It looks like (there, they're, their) in better shape than others in the neighborhood.

   _____

5. "Pile the fallen tree limbs over (there, they're, their)," said my friends' father.

   _____

Its and *It's*

Do not confuse the words *its* and *it's*. They sound the same, but they have different spellings and meanings.

Its means "belonging to it."	The dog hides in **its** bed during a storm.
It's is a contraction of *it is* or *it has*.	The storm was fierce, but now **it's** over.

Thinking Question
Which word makes sense in the sentence?

Complete each sentence with *its* or *it's*. Write the correct sentence on the line.

1. The storm did lots of damage on (its, it's) way through town.

   _____

2. The news said that (its, it's) been twenty years since we've had such a terrible storm.

   _____

3. The town garage had (its, it's) roof collapse.

   _____

4. The school district says all of (its, it's) school buses are stuck in the parking lot.

   _____

5. At my house, the snow is so deep that (its, it's) drifted up to our windows.

   _____

Kinds of Verbs

Action Verb	Helping Verb and Main Verb
I <u>enjoy</u> thunderstorms.	The cats <u>are running</u> in from the storm.

1–4. Underline the action verb in each sentence.

1. Little balls of ice battered everything in yesterday's hailstorm.

2. The hail broke several windows around town.

3. Cars suffer more damage than other things in a hailstorm.

4. Now, little round dents cover the top of our car.

5–8. Underline the helping verb once and the main verb twice.

5. Jamie is reading an article about extreme weather.

6. He has collected many books about storms.

7. For school, he will be writing a paper on lightning storms.

8. His science teacher had approved his topic last fall.

**9–10. Combine each pair of sentences to make one sentence
with a compound predicate. Write the sentence on the line.**

9. The rain pours down. It soaks everyone.

_____

10. People in the desert suffer heat during the day. They enjoy cooler temperatures
    at night.

_____

Name _____ Date _____

Lesson 11
READER'S NOTEBOOK

Hurricanes: Earth's
Mightiest Storms
Grammar: Connect to Writing

Conventions

Use the correct words to make your writing clear. Avoid being confused by words that sound the same but have different spellings and meanings.	
to, too, two	I am going **to** Jenna's house before the storm. Shani will come **too.** The weather report says we have about **two** hours before the storm hits.
there, they're, their	**There** are the umbrellas. **They're** going to come in handy today! Jenna and Shani are wearing **their** rain boots.
its, it's	Check the car to make sure **its** windows are closed. It's going to be a very rainy day!

1–10. Circle the correct word in parentheses.

1. "Did you see the lightning over (there, they're)?" Shani asked.

2. "Yes, and I heard the thunder, (two, too)," I replied.

3. Shani thinks (its, it's) exciting to watch thunderstorms.

4. Jenna likes storms (too, two).

5. Jenna and Shani have agreed that (their, they're) going to stay on the porch and watch the storm come in.

6. The porch has glass windows, and (it's, its) roof will protect them from rain.

7. I really would rather go (too, to) the movies and avoid the storm!

8. However, those (two, to) are my friends, so I will watch the storm with them.

9. Maybe I will begin to agree with (there, their) opinion of storms.

10. (Its, It's) been a long time since I watched a storm.

Focus Trait: Ideas

Vivid Details

Use strong reasons and vivid details to support your opinion and make your writing more persuasive.

Reason	Vivid Detail
Hurricanes bring winds and rain that cause terrible damage.	The wind howls like an angry monster and tosses things around. Metal scrapes along the roads like nails on a chalkboard. Rain lashes everything and turns streets into rivers.

A. Fill in the blank with the title of your favorite book. Then write two vivid supporting details that would help persuade others that the book is good.

My favorite book is _____

I like this book because _____

Vivid supporting detail: _____

_____

Vivid supporting detail: _____

_____

B. Work with a partner. Choose the kind of storm you think is the most dangerous. Work together to write a paragraph to persuade others to agree. Start an opinion statement about the type of storm. Add your main reason for your opinion. Then include at least two vivid details that support your reason.

_____

_____

_____

_____

_____

_____

The Earth Dragon Awakes

Ah Sing's Journal

Chin's father, Ah Sing, wrote in his journal describing the events of April 18, 1906. Use details from the story to infer what Chin's father may have been thinking as the earthquake unfolded.

Reread pages 350–351. Then use the sentence starters to complete this journal entry.

Wednesday, April 19, 1906

I was washing up yesterday with my son when ...

_____

_____

_____

Reread pages 354–355. Then continue the journal entry.

The worst had happened.

_____

_____

_____

Reread pages 356–357. Then continue the journal entry.

Chin started to panic...

_____

_____

_____

_____

If Ah Sing could speak to the Earth Dragon, what do you think he would say to it? Support your idea with what you know about Ah Sing's character.

_____

_____

_____

_____

Name _____ Date _____

Synonyms

> damaged   dangerous   flee   protective
> daring   wobbles   frightened

Read each sentence. Rewrite each sentence by using one of the synonyms above in place of the underlined word or words.

1. The <u>brave</u> warrior led his troops in battle.

   _____

2. We practiced how to <u>escape</u> if there was a fire in the school.

   _____

3. Some parts of the world experience <u>harmful</u> earthquakes.

   _____

4. The vase was <u>broken</u> during the move.

   _____

5. My older brother is very <u>caring</u> for me.

   _____

6. During a storm, my dog is <u>scared</u> by the thunder.

   _____

7. During an earthquake, the ground <u>shakes</u>.

   _____

Words with *-ed* or *-ing*

Basic 1–10. Complete the puzzle by writing the Basic Word for each clue.

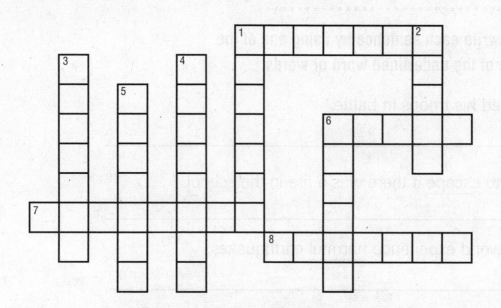

Spelling Words

1. rising
2. traced
3. stripped
4. slammed
5. dancing
6. striped
7. winning
8. snapping
9. bragging
10. handled
11. dripped
12. begged
13. dared
14. skipped
15. hitting
16. spotted
17. raced
18. dimmed
19. spinning
20. escaped

Challenge
urged
striving
whipped
breathing
quizzed

Across

1. fell in drops
6. rushed at top speed
7. shutting with a click
8. gaining a victory

Down

1. moving to music
2. challenged
3. punching or slapping
4. boasting
5. a lined pattern
6. going up

Challenge 11–14. Your class had a spelling bee yesterday. Write a short paragraph about it for your school paper. Use four of the Challenge Words. Write on a separate sheet of paper.

Spelling Word Sort

Write each Basic Word beside the correct heading.

Adding -ed: final e dropped	**Basic Words:** **Challenge Words:**
Adding -ing: final e dropped	**Basic Words:** **Challenge Words:** **Possible Selection Words:**
Adding -ed: final consonant doubled	**Basic Words:** **Challenge Words:** **Possible Selection Words:**
Adding -ing: final consonant doubled	**Basic Words:** **Possible Selection Words:**

Spelling Words

1. rising
2. traced
3. stripped
4. slammed
5. dancing
6. striped
7. winning
8. snapping
9. bragging
10. handled
11. dripped
12. begged
13. dared
14. skipped
15. hitting
16. spotted
17. raced
18. dimmed
19. spinning
20. escaped

Challenge
urged
striving
whipped
breathing
quizzed

Challenge Add the Challenge Words to your Word Sort.

Connect to Reading Look through "The Earth Dragon Awakes." Find words that have -ed or -ing. Add them to your Word Sort.

Name _____ Date _____

Proofreading for Spelling

Find the misspelled words and circle them. Write them correctly on the lines below.

Spelling Words

1. rising
2. traced
3. stripped
4. slammed
5. dancing
6. striped
7. winning
8. snapping
9. bragging
10. handled
11. dripped
12. begged
13. dared
14. skipped
15. hitting
16. spotted
17. raced
18. dimmed
19. spinning
20. escaped

Challenge
urged
striving
whipped
breathing
quizzed

My grandfather beged his parents to let him leave home to see the world. When they finally agreed, my grandfather began danceing and spining across the spoted rug in the living room. He escapt disaster as he nearly slamed into the wall. But with excitement in the air, he skiped dinner and racd upstairs to get his suitcase. He packed some pants and his favorite stiped shirts.

He was a young man when he left his home in Peru, South America. My grandfather handld all his own travel arrangements, and before he left, he tracid a map for his parents, showing the route the steamship would be traveling. For twenty-one days he did not see land. When the lights on the steamship dimed, my grandfather sat and thought about his future. The steamship arrived in San Francisco on the day of the big earthquake.

1. _____
2. _____
3. _____
4. _____
5. _____
6. _____

7. _____
8. _____
9. _____
10. _____
11. _____
12. _____

Singular Possessive Nouns

A **singular possessive noun** shows ownership by one person or thing. Add -'s to a singular noun to make it possessive.

singular possessive noun
the Earth Dragon's anger

Thinking Question
What word shows ownership by one person or thing?

1–8. Write each phrase another way. Use the possessive form of the underlined noun.

1. the father of <u>Chin</u>   _____ father

2. the son of <u>Ah Sing</u>   _____ son

3. the rumble of an <u>earthquake</u>   an _____ rumble

4. the shout of a <u>person</u>   a _____ shout

5. the courage of a <u>father</u>   a _____ courage

6. the fear of the <u>boy</u>   the _____ fear

7. the help of a <u>friend</u>   a _____ help

8. the smile of the <u>rescuer</u>   the _____ smile

Name _____ Date _____

Lesson 12
READER'S NOTEBOOK

The Earth Dragon Awakes
Grammar:
Possessive Nouns

Plural Possessive Nouns

> A **plural possessive noun** shows ownership by more than one person or thing. When a plural noun ends with -s, add only an apostrophe to make it possessive. When a plural noun does not end in -s, add an apostrophe and -s to make it possessive.
>
> **plural possessive noun**
> the dragons' caves   the men's stories

Thinking Question
What word shows ownership by more than one person or thing?

1–6. Write each phrase another way. Use the possessive form of the underlined noun.

1. legends of <u>different countries</u>

   different _____ legends

2. the long necks of <u>the sea serpents</u>

   the _____ long necks

3. the footprints of <u>the children</u>

   the _____ footprints

4. the huge wings <u>of the dragons</u>

   the _____ huge wings

5. the brave actions <u>of the young women</u>

   the _____ brave actions

6. the towers <u>of the castles</u>

   the _____ towers

Name _____ Date _____

Apostrophes in Possessive Nouns

Some plural nouns do not end in *-s*. To make these plural nouns possessive, add *-'s*.

plural possessive nouns
her feet's soles   his teeth's braces

1–8. Write each phrase another way. Use the possessive form of the underlined noun.

1. the choice of the people _____

2. the soft wool belonging to the sheep _____

3. the nests belonging to the mice _____

4. the tracks of the deer _____

5. the annoying honks of the geese _____

6. the stubbornness of the oxen _____

7. the colored fins belonging to fish _____

8. the safety of the children _____

Progressive Verb Tenses

Present Progressive Tense	is quaking
Past Progressive Tense	was quaking
Future Progressive Tense	will be quaking

1–5. Underline the progressive verb in each sentence. Write *present progressive*, *past progressive*, or *future progressive* for each verb.

1. Scientists are studying the San Andreas Fault. _____

2. In science class, I am learning that this fault causes many earthquakes.

_____

3. This week alone several small earthquakes will be occurring there.

_____

4. A few years ago, Southern California was experiencing a very strong earthquake.

_____

5. People in the area were moving to safe places.

_____

6–9. Correct this paragraph. There are four mistakes in verb tense. Write the correct progressive verbs on the lines below.

 In class yesterday, we <u>are listening</u> to an old eyewitness radio account of an earthquake. During the earthquake, the reporter said, "The ground <u>will be shaking</u> so violently that I can hardly stand up. Residents <u>were fleeing</u> the scene!" After the earthquake stopped, he said, "People <u>were returning</u> tomorrow to start rebuilding their homes."

6. _____   8. _____

7. _____   9. _____

Ideas

You can use possessive nouns to make details clearer by
showing ownership.

Unclear Detail	Clear Detail
The siren was louder than the cries.	The siren was louder than my baby brother's cries.

1–6. Rewrite each sentence to show ownership of the underlined
word or words by the noun in parentheses. Write the new sentence on
the line.

1. The tornado siren frightened our visitors. (town)

   _____

2. The loud, shrill sound made the windows rattle. (house)

   _____

3. Jacob said we should hurry to the shelter. (neighbors)

   _____

4. The shelter is a basement room with emergency supplies. (people)

   _____

   _____

5. My uncle entertained us with songs while we waited for the all-clear

   signal. (artists)

   _____

   _____

6. The music helped everyone to relax, even the dog. (my brother)

   _____

Focus Trait: Ideas
Connecting Opinions and Reasons

When you write a problem-solution paragraph, follow these steps:

1. State the problem clearly.
2. Explain why you think it is a problem.
3. Give a possible solution.
4. Use facts and details to provide reasons for that solution.
5. Clearly connect supporting facts and details to your opinion with words and phrases.

Think of a problem that you can help to fix. Complete the outline for a problem-solution paragraph. Use linking words when possible.

1. Problem: _____
   _____

2. Reason: _____
   _____

3. Possible solution: _____
   _____

   a. Fact/example: _____
   _____

   b. Fact/example: _____

4. My solution: _____
   _____

Name _____ Date _____

Lesson 13
READER'S NOTEBOOK

**Antarctic Journal:
Four Months at the
Bottom of the World**
Independent Reading

Reader's Guide

Antarctic Journal: Four Months at the Bottom of the World

Don't Try This at Home!

On December 24, the author of the *Antarctic Journal* found
herself in a very dangerous situation. Find the journal entry
and reread it. Then answer the questions below.

How is the text for this entry structured, or organized?

_____

_____

What is the author's problem in this section?

_____

_____

What can you infer happened to cause the author to fall?
What details help you make this inference?

_____

_____

_____

What does the author do to solve her problem? How does
she make sure she gets out of the glacier safely?

_____

_____

_____

_____

What do you think a tour guide would tell the author she did wrong?

_____

_____

_____

Lesson 13
READER'S NOTEBOOK

**Antarctic Journal:
Four Months at the
Bottom of the World**
Independent Reading

Suppose that you are the author and are writing the introduction to *Antarctic Journal*. Write an introduction to the book in which you:

- use main ideas and details to give a brief overview of the contents of the book,
- tell how the book is structured and why you structured it that way, and
- explain the dangers of visiting Antarctica and warn readers to follow the rules if they visit.

Introduction

_____

_____

_____

_____

_____

_____

_____

_____

_____

_____

_____

_____

_____

_____

_____

Greek and Latin Word Parts
spect, struct, tele, vis

Each word in the box comes from a Greek or Latin word. *Spect* means "look," *vis* means "see," *struct* means "build," and *tele* means "far away." Use the meanings of the Greek and Latin word parts to help you understand the meanings of the words.

respect	instruct	telescope	vision
inspected	visible	television	construction

Complete each sentence using one of the words from the box above. Write the correct word on the line.

1. We used a _____ to see the planet Jupiter.

2. The class watched an interesting program on _____ .

3. The teacher will _____ us on what to do in a fire drill.

4. Be polite and show _____ to all people.

5. Germs are small and only _____ with a microscope.

6. I need glasses to correct my _____ .

7. Get your car _____ to make sure it is safe.

8. Wear a hard hat at the building _____ site.

More Words with *-ed* or *-ing*

Basic 1–11. Write the Basic Word that best replaces the underlined word or words.

1. My family likes to go <u>walking for exercise</u> on summer vacation. _____

2. We are <u>placing</u> together a plan for our next trip. _____

3. We are <u>looking for</u> information about what to do. _____

4. Last summer, we <u>journeyed</u> to a national park. _____

5. My brother and I <u>planned</u> our route. _____

6. Our mother <u>volunteered</u> to help us. _____

7. My brother had a habit of <u>rambling</u> off on his own. _____

8. Mom was <u>starting to get</u> worried, but he returned. _____

9. We may try <u>going to</u> the lake! _____

10. My dad is <u>calling</u> ahead for cabin reservations. _____

11. I am <u>inspecting</u> our raft for leaks. _____

Challenge 12–14. Write a short paragraph about having dinner and then playing a game with your family or friends. Use three of the Challenge Words. Write on a separate sheet of paper.

Spelling Words

1. wiped
2. covered
3. mapped
4. pleasing
5. slipped
6. putting
7. traveled
8. seeking
9. visiting
10. mixed
11. shipped
12. phoning
13. offered
14. smelling
15. hiking
16. checking
17. fainted
18. landed
19. becoming
20. wandering

Challenge
amusing
entertained
admitted
stunning
starving

Spelling Word Sort

Write each Basic Word beside the correct heading.

-ed: no spelling change	**Basic Words:** **Challenge Words:** **Possible Selection Words:**
-ing: no spelling change	**Basic Words:**
-ed: final *e* dropped	**Basic Words:** **Possible Selection Words:**
-ing: final *e* dropped	**Basic Words:** **Challenge Words:** **Possible Selection Words:**
-ed: final consonant doubled	**Basic Words:** **Challenge Words:** **Possible Selection Words:**
-ing: final consonant doubled	**Basic Words:** **Challenge Words:** **Possible Selection Words:**

Spelling Words

1. wiped
2. covered
3. mapped
4. pleasing
5. slipped
6. putting
7. traveled
8. seeking
9. visiting
10. mixed
11. shipped
12. phoning
13. offered
14. smelling
15. hiking
16. checking
17. fainted
18. landed
19. becoming
20. wandering

Challenge
amusing
entertained
admitted
stunning
starving

Challenge   Add the Challenge Words to your Word Sort.

Connect to Reading   Look through "Antarctic Journal." Find words that have *-ed* or *-ing*. Add them to your Word Sort.

Name _____ Date _____

Proofreading for Spelling

Find the misspelled words and circle them. Write them correctly on the lines below.

I liked smeling the fresh coffee while I miksed pancake batter and the blueberries that were shiped to Palmer Station. As I was mixing one day, I heard a loud rumbling noise. Before I could go outside to investigate, I had to put on my parka, a wool hat, and boots. I also coverd my face with sunscreen and grabbed my sunglasses because I didn't want to risk a bad sunburn or snow blindness. My sunglasses were dirty and needed to be wipet. They landded on the snow when I was out wandereng around and sliped on the ice last night. My friends thought I'd faintted, but that was not the case. I am new here and hikeing on open ground is a bit tricky.

When I got outside, I saw a big blue whale and a newborn calf exhaling a blast of hot wet air. It was such a pleaseing sight! I really enjoy visitting new places!

1. _____   7. _____
2. _____   8. _____
3. _____   9. _____
4. _____   10. _____
5. _____   11. _____
6. _____   12. _____

Spelling Words

1. wiped
2. covered
3. mapped
4. pleasing
5. slipped
6. putting
7. traveled
8. seeking
9. visiting
10. mixed
11. shipped
12. phoning
13. offered
14. smelling
15. hiking
16. checking
17. fainted
18. landed
19. becoming
20. wandering

Challenge
amusing
entertained
admitted
stunning
starving

May, Might, Can, and Could

Modal Auxiliary	What It Expresses	Examples
may	permission to do an action; possibility that an action will happen	My parents said my sister **may** go on the field trip. She **may** see penguins in the arctic exhibit.
might	possibility that an action will happen	The class **might** also see polar bears.
can	certain ability to do an action	We **can** go on Tuesday or Thursday.
could	possibility of having the ability to do an action	Perhaps we **could** also visit the desert exhibit.

Thinking Questions
Which word is a helping verb? Does it tell about the certainty of the action?

1–5. Complete each sentence by writing a modal auxiliary from the chart.

1. Whenever it snows, Chantal _____ watch the snow fall from her window.

2. She wonders whether she _____ visit the Arctic some day.

3. Her parents have said she _____ go after she graduates from high school.

4. Chantal thinks she _____ work hard and save enough money for a trip.

5. She _____ imagine how exciting it would be to see a polar bear.

Name _____ Date _____

Would, Should, and *Must*

Modal Auxiliary	What It Expresses	Examples
would	willingness to do an action	I would go to Antarctica if I had the chance.
should	the action probably ought to happen	People going to Antarctica should learn about the area before they go.
must	the action absolutely has to happen	Visitors to Antarctica must go with an experienced guide.

Thinking Questions
Which word is a helping verb? Does it express the writer's feelings or opinion?

1–6. Complete each sentence by writing a modal auxiliary from the chart.

1. You _____ hear my uncle talk about his work in Antarctica.

2. If he ever goes back, I _____ love to go with him.

3. Before he will let me go, he says, I _____ take special training to know what to expect there.

4. Also, he thinks I _____ work hard to be in good physical shape.

5. Of course, I _____ get my parents' permission to go!

6. I _____ really enjoy seeing all that ice and visiting penguins in their natural habitat!

Using Modal Auxiliaries

Modal Auxiliary	What It Expresses
may	Someone has permission to do an action.
should	I think the action probably ought to happen.
must	I think the action absolutely needs to happen.
can	Someone has the ability to do an action.
will	This forms a future tense.

Thinking Question
Which modal auxiliary helps express my idea clearly?

1–4.   Circle the modal auxiliary in parentheses that clearly expresses the idea in the sentence.

1. Today our teacher told us that we (may, must) write our term papers on Antarctica.

2. "You all (will, can) do research at the library or online, so use whichever you prefer," our teacher said.

3. "Everyone (should, will) choose a specific topic and begin researching by Tuesday," she advised.

4. According to the assignment sheet, we (can, may) write about the weather, the land, or the animals in Antarctica.

5–6.   Write a modal auxiliary on the line that best expresses the idea.

5. To do my best on this report, I _____ find a topic I want to learn about.

6. Tomorrow, I _____ ask whether I may write about scientific expeditions to Antarctica.

Compound and Complex Sentences

For compound sentences, use a comma and coordinating conjunction to join two simple sentences. Use *and* to join ideas together, *but* to show a contrast, and *or* to show a choice.	The man arrived at the cabin, **and** his dog came with him. They could walk, **or** they could swim before dark. Swimming would be fun, **but** the weather was too cold.
For complex sentences, use a subordinating conjunction to join a simple sentence and a clause.	The dog loves winter walks **because** he enjoys the snow. **Since** snow was about to fall, the man and his dog took a short walk.

1–3. **For these compound sentences, write the conjunction that has the purpose shown in parentheses. Add a comma (,) before the conjunction.**

1. (join together) Clouds are forming _____ snow will fall.

2. (show contrast) The temperature rises _____ the wind blows harder.

3. (show choice) Will Milo get home in time _____ will Ed fall asleep first?

4–6. **For each complex sentence, underline the simple sentence once and the clause twice. Circle the subordinating conjunction.**

4. When the blizzard hits, everyone stays snug indoors.

5. Although Milo loves snow, he sleeps by the fireplace during snowstorms.

6. The cabin doors and windows rattle because the wind is so strong.

Conventions

Modal Auxiliary	What It Expresses	Examples
can	present ability	I can walk with snowshoes.
could	past ability present possibility	Years ago, people could only travel to Antarctica by ship. I could go there next year, if I wanted to.
will	willingness future tense	I will help you plan your trip. The expedition will leave in October.
would	usual activity willingness	Explorers would travel by sled over dangerous ice. Would you do that?

1–7. **Complete each sentence by writing a helping verb from the chart.**

1. _____ you like to be an explorer?

2. Today's explorers _____ venture beneath the sea or into space.

3. In the past, Arctic explorers _____ take many risks.

4. These brave men and women _____ not shelter in warm buildings.

5. By contrast, today's explorers _____ control temperatures even in space.

6. Next year, a new expedition _____ set out for the deep sea.

7. In this century, travelers _____ vacation at the South Pole!

Focus Trait: Voice
Persuasive Letter

Inappropriate Tone	Formal, Polite Tone
You should go see the snowmen and ice sculptures.	I'd like to invite you to see the snowmen and ice sculptures with me.

A. Read the parts of a letter below. On the line, rewrite each part using a more polite, formal tone.

Inappropriate Tone	Formal, Polite Tone
1. Hey Maria,	_____
2. Want to go to the museum?	I hope you will join _____ _____
3. There's a thing about Antarctica.	_____ on Antarctica.

B. Rewrite each sentence using a more formal, polite tone. Add or take out words, use synonyms, or change the sentence structure.

Pair/Share Work with a partner to come up with reasons to go to the museum.

Inappropriate Tone	Formal, Polite Tone
4. You enjoy penguins. There are some at the museum.	
5. I heard there'll be a slide for the penguins on the first day.	

Name _____ Date _____

Lesson 14
READER'S NOTEBOOK

**The Life and Times
of the Ant**
Independent Reading

The Life and Times
of the Ant

What's the Purpose?

Suppose you are an illustrator hired to create an
illustration for one of the pages of *The Life and Times
of the Ant*. Study the illustrations on pages 416–417 and
answer the questions to help you create your illustration.

Reread page 416. What is the main idea of each paragraph?

_____

_____

Describe the illustration on pages 416–417. What does it show?
How are the ants dressed?

_____

_____

How does the illustration on these pages help you understand
the main idea of the section?

_____

_____

What is the author's purpose in showing this illustration?

_____

_____

Name _____ Date _____

Lesson 14
READER'S NOTEBOOK

**The Life and Times
of the Ant**
Independent Reading

Draw an illustration that demonstrates the author's main purpose in writing *The Life and Times of the Ant.* Label important parts of the illustration and write a caption for it.

Name _____ Date _____

Lesson 14
READER'S NOTEBOOK

The Life and Times
of the Ant
Vocabulary Strategies:
Suffixes *-able, -ible*

Suffixes *-able, -ible*

edible   changeable   collapsible
agreeable   visible   breakable

**Each sentence below includes a word with the suffix *-ible* or *-able*.
Complete each sentence.**

1. A plastic apple is not edible because

   _____

2. One thing that can be described as collapsible is

   _____

3. The most agreeable people are the ones who

   _____

4. One example of changeable weather is snow on one day and

   _____

5. Something that is visible in the night sky is

   _____

6. One thing that is breakable is

   _____

Name _____ Date _____

Final Long *e*

Basic 1–10. Complete the puzzle by writing the Basic Word for each clue.

Spelling Words

1. turkey
2. lonely
3. colony
4. steady
5. hungry
6. valley
7. hockey
8. starry
9. melody
10. movie
11. duty
12. drowsy
13. chimney
14. plenty
15. daily
16. alley
17. fifty
18. empty
19. injury
20. prairie

Challenge
envy
fiery
mercy
discovery
mystery

Across

2. sleepy
5. unoccupied
6. grassland
8. starving
9. music
10. constant

Down

1. a hurt or wound
2. responsibility
3. full of stars
4. a lot
7. smokestack

Challenge 12–14. Write a story about a detective working on a case. Use three of the Challenge Words. Write on a separate sheet of paper.

Spelling Word Sort

Write each Basic Word beside the correct heading.

Final /ē/ spelled *y*	**Basic Words:** **Challenge Words:** **Possible Selection Words:**
Final /ē/ spelled *ey*	**Basic Words:**
Other spellings for final /ē/	**Basic Words:**

Spelling Words

1. turkey
2. lonely
3. colony
4. steady
5. hungry
6. valley
7. hockey
8. starry
9. melody
10. movie
11. duty
12. drowsy
13. chimney
14. plenty
15. daily
16. alley
17. fifty
18. empty
19. injury
20. prairie

Challenge
envy
fiery
mercy
discovery
mystery

Challenge Add the Challenge Words to your Word Sort.

Connect to Reading Look through "The Life and Times of the Ant." Find words that have the final /ē/ spelling patterns on this page. Add them to your Word Sort.

Proofreading for Spelling

Name _____ Date _____

READER'S NOTEBOOK

The Life and Times
of the Ant
Spelling: Final Long *e*

Find the misspelled words and circle them. Write them correctly on the lines below.

How would you like to share your bedroom with not one but fiftie or more of your closest friends? It might be crowded, but one thing is for sure—you wouldn't be lonelie. The underground nest of some ants can house up to 10 million ants. A colonie of ants can be found in many places—in an allie or in a valey. Ants love to feed on dead termites, caterpillars, and insects. They will eat the crumbs from your turky sandwich. These are some of the useful functions in the environment that hungery ants perform dayily. The next time you have some free time, instead of watching football or hocky on TV, try watching a movey about ants to learn more about these fascinating creatures!

1. _____   6. _____
2. _____   7. _____
3. _____   8. _____
4. _____   9. _____
5. _____ 10. _____

Spelling Words

1. turkey
2. lonely
3. colony
4. steady
5. hungry
6. valley
7. hockey
8. starry
9. melody
10. movie
11. duty
12. drowsy
13. chimney
14. plenty
15. daily
16. alley
17. fifty
18. empty
19. injury
20. prairie

Challenge
envy
fiery
mercy
discovery
mystery

Name _____ Date _____

Present Participles

The **present participle** of regular verbs is formed by adding -*ing* to the verb. If the verb ends in *e*, drop the *e* before adding -*ing*.

walk + ing = <u>walking</u>

move + ing = <u>moving</u>

The **participle** form of a verb can be used as an adjective.

The <u>crawling</u> ants look very busy.

Their <u>scurrying</u> bodies are all over the grass.

Thinking Question
Which verb form ending in -ing *describes a noun?*

1–8. On the line, write the present participle form of the verb shown in parentheses.

1. The (forage) _____ ants ran for cover from the rain.

2. Their (shelter) _____ nest keeps the rain out.

3. The (tower) _____ anthill is really something to see!

4. The (shift) _____ walls of the nest are not sturdy.

5. Last week, a (feast) _____ armadillo ate many ants.

6. Its (project) _____ nose dug them out.

7. Today, (harvest) _____ ants are gathering leaves.

8. Their (slice) _____ jaws cut leaves.

Past Participles

Form the **past participle** of regular verbs by adding
-*ed* to the verb. If the verb ends in *e*, drop the *e*
before adding -*ed*. If the verb ends in *y*, drop the *y*
and add -*ied*.

present	past participle
mix	mixed
store	stored
study	studied

Remember that the participle form of a verb can be
used as an adjective.

Workers move <u>stored</u> eggs each day.
The ants must move to an <u>expanded</u> nest.

> **Thinking Question**
> Which verb form that
> tells about a past action
> modifies a noun?

1–8. On the line, write the past participle form of the verb shown
in parentheses.

1. (chew) _____ dirt and saliva form little bricks for ant tunnels.

2. (pack) _____ dirt outside the tunnels forms an anthill.

3. Its (curve) _____ roof traps heat from the sun.

4. (exchange) _____ food bonds the ants of the colony.

5. A (damage) _____ nest calls for extra work.

6. The (tire) _____ ants keep working.

7. A totally (ruin) _____ nest means starting over.

8. Workers can put any (rescue) _____ larvae in the new nest.

Participial Phrases

A **participial phrase** begins with a participle and describes a noun.

Participial phrases are formed using past and present participles.

The children <u>playing with the puppy</u> leaped for joy.
Mariella returned to find her picnic lunch <u>covered with ants.</u>

Thinking Question
Which phrase contains a participle that tells about a subject?

1–5. **Underline the participial phrase in each sentence.**

1. Ants scurrying through the grass are in search of food.

2. Ants chewing on dirt are expanding their nest.

3. Ants working on their nest are ignored by the people above them.

4. Leafcutter ants have jaws adapted for cutting leaves.

5. Leaf parts carried in their jaws arrive back at the nest.

6–8. **Write a participle based on the word in the parentheses to complete each participial phrase.**

6. Ants (nest) _____ beneath the rocks were left alone.

7. Ants often do not escape alive from a nest (disturb) _____ by an anteater.

8. A picnic (invade) _____ by ants is an unhappy scene.

Name _____ Date _____

Lesson 14
READER'S NOTEBOOK

The Life and Times
of the Ant
Grammar: Spiral Review

Frequently Confused Words

Some words sound the same but have very different meanings.
These similar-sounding words are often confused.

ant, aunt	My **aunt** saw an **ant** crawling through her kitchen.
feat, feet	Jumping twelve **feet** in the air would be an amazing **feat**.
flea, flee	The dog tried to **flee** from the **flea** that was biting it.
knew, new	Bill **knew** the ants would build a **new** nest.
wait, weight	I can't **wait** until I am strong enough to lift a hundred-pound **weight**.
weather, whether	**Whether** we go camping depends on the **weather**.

1–5.   Circle the correct word in parentheses to complete the sentence.

1. I never (knew, new) until now that some insects are like superheroes.

2. A (flea, flee) can jump over 100 times its height!

3. The tiny ant can carry an object with a (wait, weight) five times its own.

4. How does such a tiny insect perform such a (feat, feet)?

5. These insects change the Earth (weather, whether) we observe them or not.

**6–11.   Circle the words that are incorrect. Write the correct
words on the blanks at the right.**

Their is probably no insect more amazing than the aunt.   _____

They make up only about 1.3 percent of the known insect   _____

species, but they account for half the total wait of all insects on   _____

Earth. They carry most of the dead bodies of tiny animals back   _____

too their nests. They move more soil than earthworms. Its true   _____

that we need ants more than they need us, weather we admit it   _____

or not.

Sentence Fluency

> You can combine sentences with participles to make them more varied and interesting.
>
> The people were watching the ants. They were curious.
> The people <u>watching</u> the ants were curious.
>
> Rosa stood up. Her arm was covered with ants.
> Her arm <u>covered</u> with ants, Rosa stood up.

1–5. Combine the sentences using participles. Use correct punctuation and capitalization. Write the sentence on the line.

1. We are learning about ants. We find them interesting.

_____

2. The ant is one of the strongest creatures on Earth. It can lift five times its weight.

_____

_____

3. We created a proposal. We hope to buy an ant farm for our class.

_____

4. We will become keen observers. We will improve our science skills.

_____

5. We will properly care for our ant farm. It will be a great addition to our class.

_____

Focus Trait: Organization
Ordering Important Details

Unordered Details	Ordered Details
A honeybee's legs carry pollen to the plants that the bee visits. The legs of a honeybee allow it to do much more than walk. Like all insects, a honeybee has six legs.	Like all insects, a honeybee has six legs. The legs of a honeybee, however, allow it to do much more than walk. Its legs also carry pollen to the plants that the bee visits.

Read each main idea. Number the details below to show the order that best supports the main idea. Write the number on the line.

Main idea: It is easy to identify a honeybee.

_____ A honeybee's body is about half an inch long.

_____ A honeybee's body has three parts.

_____ Its body is hairy, and it is yellow and black in color.

_____ Like many insects, honeybees have four wings.

Main idea: Honeybees are important insects.

_____ Pollen must move from plant to plant so new plants can grow.

_____ Honeybees help farmers produce billions of dollars worth of crops.

_____ Honeybees help plants grow by carrying pollen from one plant to another.

_____ Honeybees pollinate many food crops, such as apples, nuts, cucumbers, and cherries.

Ecology for Kids

Eco-Friendly Lodge Brochure

Take a close look at this paragraph from page 450. What words help you understand the author's argument? Circle the words that are powerful. For example, *protect* is a much stronger word than *help*. Circle the word *protect*.

One important way to protect the environment is to help stop pollution. Here are a few ideas:

Put trash in its place. Trash does not belong in the streets, rivers, or the oceans. Trash and other kinds of pollution harm all living things.

Use solar-powered clocks and calculators when you can. If you use battery-power, recycle used batteries.

When you leave a room, turn off the light. When you are not using televisions, radios, and computers, turn them off, too. That way, your family will use less electricity and save money.

Evaluate the author's word choice. How could he have made his argument even more powerful?

_____

_____

Now fill in this travel brochure for an Eco Lodge. Make sure you use words that will convince an eco-wise traveler that the lodge uses environmentally friendly practices.

 Welcome!

Paradiso Rio Rainforest Lodge is located in a protected rainforest area one hour from the capital. Our lodge offers hiking, mountain biking, horseback riding, and rainforest tours. Our rooms come with _____ faucets and showers. Our lodge has solar panels to collect _____ from the sun and convert it to _____. Our chef prepares dinners with locally grown, organic ingredients to _____ your health and the environment's. All of our practices help to make sure that your stay has no _____ on the environment!

Paradiso Rio Rainforest Lodge

Sustainable Travel

Name _____ Date _____

Using Context

crash   channel   shape   tire
track   place   thunder

Read each sentence. Circle the correct definition for each underlined word using the context of the sentence.

1. The glass fell off the table with a crash.
   a. a loud noise   **b.** a collision, a wreck

2. Everyone cheered as he ran around the track.
   a. a mark, as a footprint   **b.** a course set up for racing

3. The boat sailed down the channel.
   a. a waterway   **b.** a means of communicating

4. She didn't want anyone to take her place as she waited to buy tickets.
   a. an area or region   **b.** a position in line

5. The football player was in great shape.
   a. the outline of something **b.** physical condition

6. After we saw the lightning, we heard some thunder.
   a. to speak loudly   **b.** a loud noise from the sky

7. I could not ride my bike because there was a hole in the tire.
   a. rubber covering a wheel **b.** to run out of energy

Changing Final *y* to *i*

Basic 1–10. Write the Basic Word to complete each analogy.

1. *Trees* are to *forests* as *cities* are to _____ .

2. *Biggest* is to *largest* as *smallest* is to _____ .

3. *Weakest* is to *strongest* as *liveliest* is to _____ .

4. *Seeds* are to *plants* as *caterpillars* are to _____ .

5. *Smoother* is to *rougher* as *tougher* is to _____ .

6. *Happier* is to *merrier* as *windier* is to _____ .

7. *Better* is to *best* as _____ is to *noisiest*.

8. *Lightest* is to *darkest* as *ugliest* is to _____ .

9. *Cleaning* is to *chores* as *photography* is to _____ .

10. *Cold* is to *colder* as *busy* is to _____ .

1. _____   6. _____
2. _____   7. _____
3. _____   8. _____
4. _____   9. _____
5. _____   10. _____

Challenge 11–14. You helped out at the community garage sale. Tell how you sorted items for sale. Use four of the Challenge Words. Write on a separate sheet of paper.

Spelling Words

1. tiniest
2. hobbies
3. copied
4. countries
5. pitied
6. easier
7. laziest
8. families
9. spied
10. happiest
11. ladies
12. friendlier
13. studied
14. busier
15. breezier
16. prettiest
17. noisier
18. healthier
19. butterflies
20. funniest

Challenge
heaviest
categories
communities
multiplied
qualities

Spelling Word Sort

Ecology for Kids
Spelling: Changing Final *y* to *i*

Write each Basic Word beside the correct heading.

Adding *-es* to a consonant + *y* word	**Basic Words:**
	Challenge Words:
	Possible Selection Words:
Adding *-ed* to a consonant + *y* word	**Basic Words:**
	Challenge Words:
Adding *-er* to a consonant + *y* word	**Basic Words:**
Adding *-est* to a consonant + *y* word	**Basic Words:**
	Challenge Words:

Spelling Words

1. tiniest
2. hobbies
3. copied
4. countries
5. pitied
6. easier
7. laziest
8. families
9. spied
10. happiest
11. ladies
12. friendlier
13. studied
14. busier
15. breezier
16. prettiest
17. noisier
18. healthier
19. butterflies
20. funniest

Challenge
heaviest
categories
communities
multiplied
qualities

Challenge Add the Challenge Words to your Word Sort.

Connect to Reading Look through "Ecology for Kids." Find words that change the final *y* to *i* before adding *-es, -ed, -er,* or *-est*. Add them to your Word Sort.

Proofreading for Spelling

Ecology for Kids
Spelling: Changing Final *y* to *i*

Find the misspelled words and circle them. Write them correctly on the lines below.

Observing nature can be entertaining and informative. Nature has been speid upon and studied through the ages and has taught ladys, gentlemen, and familes many lessons. We have coiped things we see happening in nature to make us healthyer and friendlyer. We have pityd people who take no notice of nature. Some of the prettyiest and funnieste things can be found in nature—look at a sunset, or look at baby birds, each noiser than the other, opening their mouths wide to be fed. Many people have found that some of their happist times have been spent observing nature.

1. _____   7. _____
2. _____   8. _____
3. _____   9. _____
4. _____   10. _____
5. _____   11. _____
6. _____   12. _____

Spelling Words

1. tiniest
2. hobbies
3. copied
4. countries
5. pitied
6. easier
7. laziest
8. families
9. spied
10. happiest
11. ladies
12. friendlier
13. studied
14. busier
15. breezier
16. prettiest
17. noisier
18. healthier
19. butterflies
20. funniest

Challenge
heaviest
categories
communities
multiplied
qualities

Irregular Verbs

Verbs that do not add *-ed* to show past action are called **irregular verbs**. You must remember the spellings of irregular verbs.

present tense verb: give
irregular past tense verb: gave

Thinking Question
What verb does not add -ed to show past action?

1–8. Write the correct form of the verb in parentheses to show past action.

1. The scientist (know) how to protect the environment.
_____

2. Our science teacher (brings) photographs of various ecosystems to class. _____

3. She (tells) us that one way to protect the environment is to stop pollution. _____

4. It would also help the environment if we (grow) our own vegetables. _____

5. We (take) very long showers. _____

6. We (leave) the lights on in empty rooms.
_____

7. We (drive) everywhere instead of walking or riding bikes.
_____

8. My family and I (make) a plan for how to save water, electricity, and gasoline. _____

The Special Verb *be*

The verb *be* tells what someone or something is or is like. It does not show action. It can be used as a main verb or a helping verb. The verb *be* has special forms for different tenses and different subjects.

Thinking Questions
What is the subject? What is the tense? What form of be *is correct?*

forms of the verb *be*

subject	present tense	past tense
I	am	was
he, she, it	is	was
we, you, they	are	were

past participle with form of helping verb *have*

I, we, you, they	have been
he, she, it	has been

1–6. Write the form of the verb *be* in parentheses that correctly completes each sentence.

1. Last week, the students (are, were) learning about ecosystems. _____

2. An ecosystem (is, are) a place where groups of living and nonliving things interact with their environment. _____

3. Forests, lakes, and deserts (is, are) examples of ecosystems. _____

4. Yesterday, I (am, was) working on a project about the ocean. _____

5. Today, I (am, was) presenting my project about the ocean to my classmates. _____

6. I (been, have been) enjoying learning about the ocean. _____

Helping Verbs

Many **irregular verbs** change spelling when they are used with **helping verbs**. Often the new spelling uses *-n* or *-en* to show past tense.

Irregular verb: grow
Past tense: grew
Past tense form with helping verb: had grown

1–5. On the line, write the correct form of the verb in parentheses.

1. My class had (drive) _____ all morning to get to the seashore.

2. Then we had (ride) _____ in a boat to get to a mangrove swamp.

3. It was the first time I had (see) _____ such a unique ecosystem.

4. When it heard us coming, a heron had (hide) _____ among the trees.

5. Afterwards, a scientist had (speak) _____ to us about preserving mangrove swamps.

Progressive Verb Tenses

Progressive verb tenses show action that is ongoing.

present progressive	is learning, are learning
past progressive	was learning, were learning
future progressive	will be learning

1–7. **Complete each sentence with the correct progressive form of the verb in parentheses ( ).**

1. Our planet _____ more polluted every year. (become)

2. Tropical rainforests _____ rapidly now. (disappear)

3. Two hundred years ago, these forests _____ on four different continents. (thrive)

4. But the need for land to settle _____ rapidly. (grow)

5. Settlers _____ forests to raise crops. (clear)

6. Now people _____ trees to replace some of our lost forests. (plant)

7. The students at our school _____ Earth Day next April. (celebrate)

Conventions

Incorrect Form of Verb
They dove into the bay and <u>taked</u> a look at its ecosystem.
Correct Form of Verb
They dove into the bay and <u>took</u> a look at its ecosystem.

**1–5.   Choose the correct form for the verb in the parentheses.
Rewrite the sentences to make the author's meaning clear.**

1. Yesterday, the scientists (find, found) an unfamiliar

creature in the bay.

_____

_____

2. When they returned to shore, they (brung, brought) it to

the laboratory.

_____

_____

3. They now (know, knew) some of the changes

that happened as a result of pollution in the bay.

_____

_____

4. The scientists (writed, wrote) a report about their findings.

_____

_____

5. They (gived, gave) a talk about their discoveries.

_____

_____

Focus Trait: Ideas
Focusing on the Main Idea

Good writers keep readers interested in their opinions by keeping
the ideas in each paragraph connected to the main idea. This
writer deleted a sentence that did not support the main idea.

Lightning is caused by electric charges. Ice and raindrops move quickly in a
storm cloud and create a charge at the bottom of the cloud. At the same time,
an opposite charge is created on the ground. When sparks from the cloud meet
sparks from the ground, they create a bolt of lightning. ~~A tree hit by a bolt of
lightning can sometimes survive.~~

    Main idea: *Lightning is caused by electric charges.*

**Read the paragraph and write the main idea. Then cross out the
sentence that does not support the main idea.**

1. A fulgarite is a long tube in the ground created by
   lightning. First, lightning hits the ground and goes deep
   into the soil. A bolt of lightning has as much power as
   all the power plants in the United States can make in the
   same amount of time! The heat from the lightning melts
   sand in the ground, forming a fulgarite. This crusty tube
   shows the shape of the lightning bolt.

Main idea: _____

2. There is a story told about Benjamin Franklin that he performed
   an experiment that is now famous. He flew a kite in a big
   storm. A key was tied to the bottom of the kite string.
   Lightning struck, and sparks flew from the key! You can
   estimate how far lightning is by listening to thunder. A silk
   ribbon on the string kept Franklin's hand from getting hurt.

Main idea: _____

Reader's Guide

Riding Freedom

You're Hired!

Authors use personification to help readers see, feel, and hear
what is being described and give color to the description. Answer
the questions below about personification in "Riding Freedom."

Reread page 480. Find an example of personification. List it below.

_____

_____

_____

What nonliving thing is the author describing? What human
characteristics does the author give to it?

_____

_____

_____

How does the author's use of personification help you better see, feel,
or sense the object? How does it help you understand it?

_____

_____

_____

_____

Imagine that Charley asks James to write a job recommendation for a driving position with a new company. Follow the steps below to help James write the recommendation.

- Reread pages 478–483.
- Think about Charley/Charlotte's performance. In what difficult circumstances did Charlotte find herself? How did she still manage to do her job? Include personification to describe how Charley prevailed.

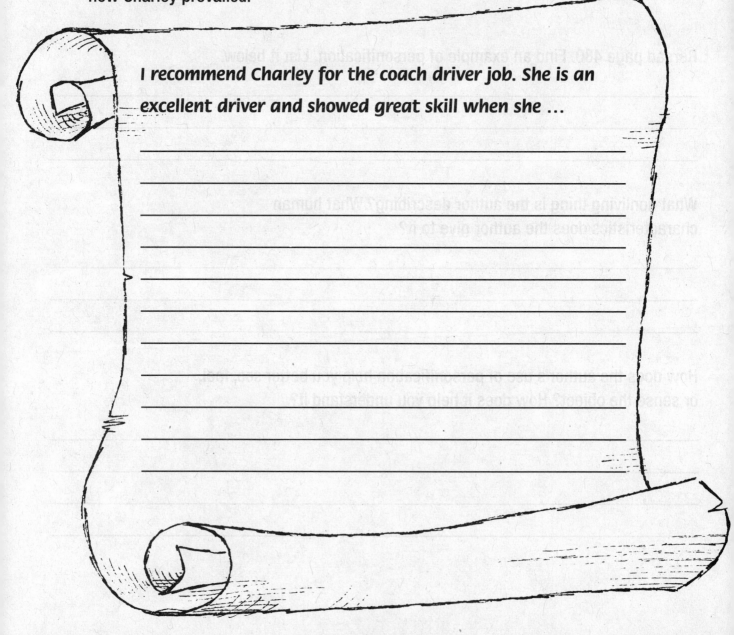

I recommend Charley for the coach driver job. She is an excellent driver and showed great skill when she ...

_____

_____

_____

_____

_____

_____

_____

_____

_____

_____

_____

Figurative Language

Figurative language describes something by comparing it to something else that seems to be unlike it.

A **simile** is figurative language that compares two things using *like* or *as*.
examples: The horse runs like the wind. The rider is as skinny as a rail.

A **metaphor** is figurative language that makes a comparison without *like* or *as*.
examples: That storm was a monster. Each snowflake is a sculpted gem.

An **idiom** is figurative language that uses words in a way other than their usual meaning.
examples: under the weather (feeling sick); to be all wet (to be totally wrong)

1–3. Circle the words that best complete each metaphor or simile. Then, on the line, write *S* if the comparison is a simile. Write *M* if it is a metaphor.

1. When the passengers changed places it was like _____.

   a. a game of musical chairs   **b.** a steep cliff

2. When the children became tired, they fought like _____.

   a. a sleeping kitten   **b.** cats and dogs

3. The rough, winding road was _____.

   a. a puzzle to solve   **b.** a field of trees

Figure out the meaning of the underlined idiom. Write the meaning on the line.

4. The passengers were <u>on edge</u> because they feared the stagecoach would be robbed. _____

Words with /k/, /ng/, and /kw/

Basic 1–11. Write the Basic Word that best replaces the underlined word or words in each sentence.

1. Some students love the <u>subject</u> of gymnastics.

2. We avoid <u>dangerous</u> gymnastic exercises.

3. Some fear making a <u>blunder</u> while performing.

4. A gymnast accidentally <u>hit</u> her feet on the balance beam.

5. Her feet will <u>hurt</u> until they're iced.

6. She will present a <u>query</u> to her coach about safety.

7. These two gymnasts have <u>the same</u> ability on the parallel bars.

8. Young gymnasts perform for the <u>community audience</u>.

9. Soon the <u>empty</u> scoreboard will show our score.

10. The scoreboard is flashing now in <u>charged</u> lights!

11. Let's have our <u>outdoor party</u> after practice.

1. _____	7. _____
2. _____	8. _____
3. _____	9. _____
4. _____	10. _____
5. _____	11. _____
6. _____	

Spelling Words

1. risky
2. track
3. topic
4. blank
5. question
6. pocket
7. monkey
8. junk
9. equal
10. ache
11. public
12. attack
13. struck
14. earthquake
15. picnic
16. banker
17. electric
18. blanket
19. mistake
20. stomach

Challenge
request
skeleton
peculiar
attic
reckless

Challenge 12–14. Write about the headline below. Use three Challenge Words. Write on a separate sheet of paper.

> **IMPORTANT ARCHAEOLOGICAL**
> **DISCOVERY MADE**

Spelling Word Sort

Write each Basic Word beside the correct heading.

/k/ spelled *ck*	Basic Words: Challenge Words: Possible Selection Words:
/k/ spelled *k* or *c*	Basic Words: Challenge Words: Possible Selection Words:
Other spellings for /k/	Basic Words:
Spellings for /kw/	Basic Words: Challenge Words:
/ng/ before *k*	Basic Words:

Spelling Words

1. risky
2. track
3. topic
4. blank
5. question
6. pocket
7. monkey
8. junk
9. equal
10. ache
11. public
12. attack
13. struck
14. earthquake
15. picnic
16. banker
17. electric
18. blanket
19. mistake
20. stomach

Challenge
request
skeleton
peculiar
attic
reckless

Challenge   Add the Challenge Words to your Word Sort.

Connect to Reading   Look through "Riding Freedom." Find words that have the /k/, /ng/, and /kw/ spelling patterns on this page. Add them to your Word Sort.

Proofreading for Spelling

Riding Freedom
Spelling: Words with /k/, /ng/,
and /kw/

Find the misspelled words and circle them. Write them correctly
on the lines below.

The stagecoach driver was glad to pull into the station
yard. It had been a riskey ride. There was always the threat
that outlaws would attak them. There was an eqal threat
of the area being struk by an earthkwake. The driver had
to leave her seat to remove some junck that obstructed the
trak. She thought it might be an ambush—but all was well.

She was carrying a special passenger—a bankar who
carried a lot of money in his pockit. This passenger was very
demanding—he even asked for an extra blankit. It all was
enough to make the driver's stomak acke!

1. _____ 7. _____

2. _____ 8. _____

3. _____ 9. _____

4. _____ 10. _____

5. _____ 11. _____

6. _____ 12. _____

Spelling Words

1. risky
2. track
3. topic
4. blank
5. question
6. pocket
7. monkey
8. junk
9. equal
10. ache
11. public
12. attack
13. struck
14. earthquake
15. picnic
16. banker
17. electric
18. blanket
19. mistake
20. stomach

Challenge
request
skeleton
peculiar
attic
reckless

Adjectives

An **adjective** is a word that gives information about a noun or pronoun. An adjective can tell *what kind* or *how many*.

A <u>sudden</u> <u>boom</u> of thunder scared the <u>six</u> <u>horses</u>. <u>drinking</u> <u>fountain</u> (fountain for drinking)

Thinking Question
What words describe a noun?

1–3. **Write the adjectives that describe the underlined nouns. Then write *what kind* or *how many* for each adjective.**

1. We saw several <u>flashes</u> of bright <u>lightning</u> across the sky.

_____

2. The frightened <u>horses</u> bolted down the steep <u>hill</u>.

_____

3. The cold, hard <u>rain</u> soaked the driver.

_____

4–6. **Write each adjective and circle the noun that it describes.**

4. Today, heavy traffic often clogs the streets of big cities.

_____

5. Drivers tied their horses to hitching posts while they ate a hot meal.

_____

6. The rough, dirt roads of the past have been replaced by smooth highways.

_____

Adjectives After *Be*

Adjectives describe nouns and pronouns such as *I*, *it*, and *we*.

An adjective can follow the word it describes. This usually happens when an adjective follows a form of the verb *be*.

She was proud.

Thinking Questions
What adjective follows a form of be? *What word does it describe?*

1–8. **Underline each adjective. Then write the word that it describes on the line.**

1. The river was deep. _____

2. I am warm under the blanket. _____

3. The driver is calm. _____

4. The valley is foggy. _____

5. We were tired from the journey. _____

6. The horses are strong. _____

7. The coach was confident. _____

8. The ride is bumpy. _____

Name _____ Date _____

Order of Adjectives

If more than one adjective tells about a noun, those adjectives must be in the correct order. Use this order for lists of adjectives:

Opinion	Size/Shape	Age/Color	Material	Purpose	Noun
gorgeous	long	old	woolen	winter	coat
skillful		young		horse	trainer

Read the sentences. Combine the adjectives in the correct order and write them on the line.

1. The jockey is an athlete.
   She is slim.
   The jockey is skillful.
   The jockey is a _____ athlete.

2. Seabiscuit was a racehorse.
   He was a thoroughbred.
   He was remarkable.
   Seabiscuit was a _____ racehorse.

3. He had a body that looked unfit for speed.
   His build was thick.
   He was awkward.
   He had a(n) _____ body that seemed unfit for speed.

4. This small horse would become the champion of all time.
   He was the greatest.
   He was beloved.
   This small horse would become one of the
   _____ champions of all time.

Modal Auxiliaries

Helping verbs are used with main verbs. Some helping verbs help express whether the action is possible, certain to happen, or should happen.

Thinking Question
What type of action is being expressed in the sentence?

Helping Verb	Expresses	Example
may, can	action is possible	That horse *can* run fast. It *may* win the race.
could, might	action is possible but not certain	If it were younger, I *could* train it to jump. The vet *might* repair the horse's broken leg.
will, must	action has to occur	Your horse *will* run, but you *must* train it.
should	opinion: what ought to happen	You *should* feed and water your horse before you rest.

Write a helping verb from the chart to complete each sentence.

1. I will show that I _____ drive a team again.

2. Frank and James believe that Charley _____ not drive again.

3. Charlotte _____ prove that she is capable or give up her work.

4. If she learns new ways of sensing the road, she _____ succeed in her goal.

5. She knows that the bridge _____ fall with heavy weight on it.

Sentence Fluency

Short, Choppy Sentences	Combined Sentences with Adjective
The stagecoach pulled up to the inn. The stagecoach was crowded.	The crowded stagecoach pulled up to the inn.

1–2. Combine each pair of sentences by moving an adjective before a noun.

1. The seats inside the coach softened the bumpy ride. The

seats were leather.

_____

_____

2. The door rattled the entire ride. The door was creaky.

_____

_____

Short, Choppy Sentences	Combined Sentences with Adjectives
The travelers were tired. They were hungry.	The travelers were tired and hungry.

3–4. Combine each pair of sentences by joining adjectives with the word *and*.

3. The old stagecoach was leaky. It was damp.

_____

_____

4. The scenery was beautiful on their journey west. The

scenery was wild.

_____

_____

Focus Trait: Ideas
Describing with Similes

Description	Description with Simile
The passengers huddled together.	The passengers huddled together like a bunch of grapes.

A. Read each description. Make it more vivid by adding a simile.
   Remember to use *like* or *as*.

Description	Description with Simile
1. The river water was cold.	The river water was _____
2. The dark clouds moved quickly.	The dark clouds moved _____

B. Read each sentence. Add a simile to each sentence to make
   the description more vivid. Write your new sentences.

Pair/Share Work with a partner to brainstorm similes to add.

Description	Simile Added
3. The river had risen.	
4. The wood of the bridge moaned.	
5. The bridge timbers swayed.	

Reader's Guide

The Right Dog for the Job: Ira's Path from Service Dog to Guide Dog

Guide Dog Timeline

Complete the timeline using details from the article.

Read page 503. Where does Ira go first?

_____

_____

Read page 508. Where does Ira go next?

_____

_____

Read page 509. Who does Ira work with next?

_____

_____

What is Ira finally ready to do?

_____

_____

Why was it important for Ira to take these steps to become a service dog? Tell why each step was important, and why the order the steps were taken is important.

_____

_____

_____

_____

_____

_____

_____

_____

_____

_____

_____

Name _____ Date _____

Lesson 17
READER'S NOTEBOOK

The Right Dog for
the Job
Vocabulary Strategies:
Suffixes -ion, -ation, -ition

Suffixes -ion, -ation, -ition

> information   exhibition   attention   graduation
> competition   combination   cooperation

**Each sentence shows a word in parentheses that uses the suffix
-ion, -ation, or -ition. Complete the sentence using the word in
parentheses.**

1. (information) When I read a newspaper _____

   _____

2. (competition) She was excited about being _____

   _____

3. (exhibition) He wanted to go see the paintings at _____

   _____

4. (combination) I think that ice cream and cake is _____

   _____

5. (attention) Yelling very loud will get you _____

   _____

6. (cooperation) When you're working in a group at school

   _____

7. (graduation) After you finish school, _____

   _____

Lesson 17
READER'S NOTEBOOK

The Right Dog for the Job
Spelling: Words with Final /j/ and /s/

Words with Final /j/ and /s/

Basic 1–11. Write the Basic Word that best completes each group.

1. preparation, training, _____

2. workplace, department, _____

3. buggy, coach, _____

4. destruction, wreckage, _____

5. observe, see, _____

6. twofold, double, _____

7. possibility, likelihood, _____

8. bundle, carton, _____

9. wedlock, matrimony, _____

10. supervise, guide, _____

11. look, peep, _____

Challenge 12–14. Describe costumes and sets you might design for a school play that takes place in medieval times. Use three Challenge Words. Write on a separate sheet of paper.

Spelling Words

1. glance
2. judge
3. damage
4. package
5. twice
6. stage
7. carriage
8. since
9. practice
10. marriage
11. baggage
12. office
13. message
14. bridge
15. chance
16. notice
17. ridge
18. manage
19. palace
20. bandage

Challenge
fringe
average
fleece
fragrance
excellence

Spelling Word Sort

Write each Basic Word beside the correct heading.

/j/ in one-syllable words	**Basic Words:** **Challenge Words:**
/ĭj/ in two-syllable words	**Basic Words:**
/ĭj/ in words with more than two syllables	**Challenge Words:**
Final /s/ spelled *ce*	**Basic Words:** **Challenge Words:** **Possible Selection Words:**

Spelling Words

1. glance
2. judge
3. damage
4. package
5. twice
6. stage
7. carriage
8. since
9. practice
10. marriage
11. baggage
12. office
13. message
14. bridge
15. chance
16. notice
17. ridge
18. manage
19. palace
20. bandage

Challenge
fringe
average
fleece
fragrance
excellence

Challenge   Add the Challenge Words to your Word Sort.

Connect to Reading   Look through "The Right Dog for the Job."
Find words that have the final /j/ and /s/ spelling patterns. Add
them to your Word Sort.

Name _____ Date _____

Lesson 17
READER'S NOTEBOOK

The Right Dog for
the Job
Spelling: Words with Final /j/
and /s/

Proofreading for Spelling

**Find the misspelled words and circle them. Write them correctly
on the lines below.**

My sister Jenny's new guide dog, Goldie, is now a
welcome member of our household. She came with very
little bagage—just one squeaky toy. We've been to the pet
store tweice sinse then, so now Goldie has a big basket of
dog toys in Jenny's offise.

Goldie's a hero, too! A few weeks ago, she and Jenny
walked along the rige behind our house. Jenny tripped and
sprained her ankle. Goldie barked for help, and a police
officer on a nearby brige heard her. He came, put a bandag
on Jenny's ankle, and helped her home.

Last week there was a guide-dog award ceremony.
The judje called Goldie and Jenny up on staje. He read a
mesage Jenny had sent describing Goldie's actions. Then
he gave Goldie a medal and Jenny a pakage with dog treats.
Goldie looked like the queen of the palase.

1. _____ 7. _____
2. _____ 8. _____
3. _____ 9. _____
4. _____ 10. _____
5. _____ 11. _____
6. _____ 12. _____

Spelling Words

1. glance
2. judge
3. damage
4. package
5. twice
6. stage
7. carriage
8. since
9. practice
10. marriage
11. baggage
12. office
13. message
14. bridge
15. chance
16. notice
17. ridge
18. manage
19. palace
20. bandage

Challenge
fringe
average
fleece
fragrance
excellence

Adverbs that Tell *How, When,* and *Where*

An **adverb** is a word that tells something about a verb. Some adverbs tell *how*, *when*, or *where*. An adverb can come before or after the verb. Most adverbs that tell *how* end in *-ly*.

The adverbs in this sentence tell about the verb *played*:

Thinking Questions
What is the verb? What word tells how about the verb?

when   **how   where**
Yesterday, our puppy played happily outside.

1–5.   The verb in each sentence is underlined. Write the adverb. Then write whether it tells *when*, *how*, or *where*.

1. Leon talked softly to the new puppy. _____
2. Robo licked Leon's face excitedly. _____
3. Suddenly, Leon hugged Robo. _____
4. Now the family plays with Robo. _____
5. Leon taught Robo to sit there. _____

6–10.   Underline each adverb. Write the verb it describes.

6. Someday Robo will learn how to behave. _____
7. He secretly chewed Dad's new slippers. _____
8. Mom put the puppy outside. _____
9. Robo wagged his tail innocently. _____
10. Everyone immediately laughed at the dog's expression.

_____

Adverbs of Frequency and Intensity

An **adverb** is a word that tells something about a verb.
Some adverbs tell how often something happens.

We <u>usually</u> walk in the park.
Ralph <u>sometimes</u> barks at birds.

Some adverbs tell how much of something is done.

He ate <u>enough</u>, but he <u>hardly</u> slept.
She <u>almost</u> won the race.

Thinking Questions
Which word is the verb? Which word tells how often or how much?

1–5. The verb in each sentence is underlined. Write the adverb that tells *how often*.

1. I always <u>take</u> my dog, Pal, for a walk. _____

2. Pal and I <u>visit</u> the dog park often. _____

3. I usually <u>make</u> him wear his leash in the park.

   _____

4. One little black dog seldom <u>barks</u>. _____

5. Pal never <u>barks</u> or bites. _____

6–10. Underline each adverb. Write the verb it describes.

6. We sometimes swim with our dogs. _____

7. Pal scarcely stopped at the water's edge. _____

8. I almost won a race with Pal. _____

9. My good dog, Pal, nearly lost that race! _____

10. Pal follows me a lot. _____

Adverbs in Different Parts of Sentences

An **adverb** is a word that tells something about a verb. Adverbs often follow the verb, though some adverbs can be used at the beginning, middle, or end of a sentence.

adverb: carefully

<u>Carefully</u>, Mrs. Marsh trained her service dog.
Mrs. Marsh <u>carefully</u> trained her service dog.
Mrs. Marsh trained her service dog <u>carefully</u>.

Thinking Questions
What is the adverb that tells about the verb? In what part of the sentence is the adverb?

1–5. The verb in each sentence is underlined. Write the adverb.

1. Often a dog trainer <u>makes</u> careless mistakes. _____

2. Puppies in their first year of life <u>learn</u> best. _____

3. A trainer <u>repeats</u> the commands again. _____

4. Our teacher usually <u>knows</u> every dog. _____

5. I <u>think</u> about my dog a lot. _____

6–10. Underline each adverb. Write the verb it describes.

6. Once, five of the guide dogs got an award. _____

7. Three of the dogs had won before. _____

8. He quickly drank all the water in his bowl. _____

9. The best guide dog works for Mrs. Hatcher now. _____

10. Spot, please come here. _____

Progressive Verb Tenses

Progressive verb tenses express continuing action. Each progressive tense is formed by joining a form of *be* with the *-ing* form of a verb.

Present Progressive: is teaching, are teaching (now)
Past Progressive: was teaching, were teaching (earlier)
Future Progressive: will be teaching (at a later time)

1–9.   Complete each sentence using the verb and progressive form in parentheses ( ).

1. The trainers _____ a new guide dog to Alisha. (giving, future)

2. Alisha _____ excitedly for the new dog. (waiting, present)

3. Her old dog _____ her until he became ill. (guiding, past)

4. The trainers _____ the new dog now. (evaluating, present)

5. They _____ sure to prepare the dog for its tasks. (make, future)

6. The dog _____ very quickly. (learn, present)

7. He already _____ for red lights. (stop, present)

8. Yesterday, Alisha _____ the application to get the dog. (filling out, past)

9. She hopes the new dog _____ her for many years. (serve, future)

Word Choice

> Good writers choose precise **adverbs**. An adverb can change the meaning of a sentence.
>
> She walked <u>painfully</u> across the street.
>
> She walked <u>lazily</u> across the street.
>
> She walked <u>proudly</u> across the street.

Read the story. Then fill in the blanks with precise adverbs. Create a story that makes sense.

My aunt Remedios is ninety years old. _____ we visited her in Arizona. Her canine companion, Charles, whined _____ when we arrived. Aunt Remy sat _____ in her wheelchair. My mother told us that she could _____ walk.

During our visit, we saw that Charles helped Remy _____ . That good dog _____ left my aunt's side. When Remy accidentally dropped something, Charles _____ picked it up in his mouth. When she rolled her chair _____ , Charles followed.

I know that Aunt Remy would be lonely without her dog. I _____ miss Charles, too.

Focus Trait: Voice
Using Informal Language

A friendly letter is written to a person you know well. You may use informal language in a friendly letter. You may often tell a story, or narrative, in a friendly letter.

Heading	450 Bond Street Lakeside, OH 12345 June 1, 2014
Salutation	Dear Grandma,
Message	Hot dog! I just opened the birthday gift you sent me. It is awesome! I love the necklace and matching bracelet. How did you know blue gemstones are my favorite? I will think of you whenever I wear the pretty jewelry. Thank you very much.
Closing **Signature**	Your loving granddaughter, Alyssa

Write a message for a thank-you note on the lines below. State the reason you are writing the letter and connect ideas in an orderly way. Write your letter as a short narrative. Use words you would in regular speech.

Dear _____

_____

_____

_____

_____

_____

Hercules' Quest

Zeus' Speech

At the end of the story, Zeus was so pleased with his son that he brought him to Mount Olympus to live with him and the other gods. Imagine Zeus wants to have an awards ceremony for his son, Hercules, to introduce him to the other gods and to his new home. Help Zeus write a speech introducing his son. Reread pages 532–536 and answer these questions to prepare you for writing the speech.

How does Hercules accomplish his first goal? What does this tell you about his character?

_____

_____

How does Hercules accomplish his second goal? What does this tell you about his character?

_____

_____

How does Hercules accomplish his third goal? What does this tell you about his character?

_____

_____

Reread the comment about the allusion "the wrath of Hera" on page 533. Think of a word that could be an allusion to Hercules. What would it mean?

_____

_____

Write Zeus's speech below. In the speech, tell how Hercules earned his position among the gods because of his acts. Include your allusion for Hercules in your speech.

Please welcome my son, Hercules! Through his great acts of
strength, he has proven he is a god.

_____

_____

_____

_____

_____

_____

_____

_____

_____

_____

_____

_____

_____

_____

_____

Name _____ Date _____

Adages and Proverbs

> Practice makes perfect.   The early bird gets the worm.
> Look before you leap.   Seeing is believing.
> Honesty is the best policy.   There's no use crying over spilt milk.

Complete each sentence using one of the sayings from the box.

1. Hercules awoke at dawn because he knew that _____

   _____ .

2. Hercules didn't lie to his father because he knew that

   _____ .

3. As a boy, Hercules acted rashly and did not know that you

   should _____

   _____ .

4. Zeus knew Hercules would someday learn to use his powers

   wisely because _____

   _____ .

5. He didn't think Hercules could kill a lion. When he watched the

   boy fight the animal, he realized that _____

   _____ .

6. Hercules didn't worry about what he had done in the past

   because _____

   _____ .

Prefixes *re-*, *un-*, *dis-*

Hercules' Quest
Spelling:
Prefixes: *re-*, *un-*, *dis-*

Basic 1–10. Read the paragraphs. Write the Basic Words that best complete the sentences.

"Look how (1) _____ this room is!" my dad said. I said that I had cleaned it earlier, but he told me that I needed to (2) _____ the whole thing. I didn't want to (3) _____ him, so I started to organize some of the (4) _____. I noticed right away that a shelf of books was sagging and (5) _____, so I decided that I would try to (6) _____ the whole bookcase. I started to (7) _____ all of the books onto the floor and took the bookcase apart. This (8) _____ task took longer than cleaning the room would have taken.

"George!" exclaimed my father. "I (9) _____ that I asked you an hour ago to clean your room!"

Now I remember why I (10) _____ cleaning so much!

Challenge 11–14. Your favorite store is going out of business. Write an e-mail to a friend about your last visit to the store. Use four Challenge Words. Write on a separate sheet of paper.

Spelling Words

1. unused
2. refresh
3. dislike
4. replace
5. unpaid
6. redo
7. disorder
8. unplanned
9. distrust
10. rewind
11. untrue
12. unload
13. recall
14. displease
15. uneven
16. rebuild
17. restart
18. uncover
19. untidy
20. discolor

Challenge
disband
rearrange
discontinue
refund
unusual

Spelling Word Sort

Write each Basic Word beside the correct heading.

re- + base word	**Basic Words:**
	Challenge Words:
dis- + base word	**Basic Words:**
	Challenge Words:
un- + base word	**Basic Words:**
	Challenge Words:

Challenge Add the Challenge Words to your Word Sort.

Spelling Words

1. unused
2. refresh
3. dislike
4. replace
5. unpaid
6. redo
7. disorder
8. unplanned
9. distrust
10. rewind
11. untrue
12. unload
13. recall
14. displease
15. uneven
16. rebuild
17. restart
18. uncover
19. untidy
20. discolor

Challenge
disband
rearrange
discontinue
refund
unusual

Name __Daneysi Lopez 8__   Date __1/12/15__

Proofreading for Spelling

Hercules' Quest
Spelling:
Prefixes: *re-, un-, dis-*

Find the misspelled words and circle them. Write them
correctly on the lines below.

To the ancient Greeks, an earthquake or drought was not
accidental or (unplaned). Everything had a reason. So, how
did they attempt to explain these events and (replaise) the
unknown with the known? They did this by telling stories
about their gods. Today we call these stories Greek myths.

Many of the Greek gods seemed to (dislieke) one
another. There was a lot of (distrussed) as they competed for
power. Humans had to be careful not to (displeaze) the gods,
for doing so could bring chaos and (dissorder). An (uneaven)
relationship existed, as some gods were kind, while others
were cruel.

Though the myths are (untrew) historians use them to
(uncuver) the truth about Greek life. Ancient stories help us
(recawl) how people lived and (rebild) the story of their society.
These ancient myths allow us to (rewinde) the human story
and see how ancient people explained difficult ideas.

Spelling Words

1. unused
2. refresh
3. dislike
4. replace
5. unpaid
6. redo
7. disorder
8. unplanned
9. distrust
10. rewind
11. untrue
12. unload
13. recall
14. displease
15. uneven
16. rebuild
17. restart
18. uncover
19. untidy
20. discolor

Challenge
disband
rearrange
discontinue
refund
unusual

1. displease
2. disorder
3. dislike
4. replace
5. rewind
6. rebuild
7. uneven
8. untrue
9. unplanned
10. uncover
11. distrust
12. recall

Name _____ Date _____

Prepositions

A **preposition** shows the connection between words in a sentence. Some prepositions describe time, such as *before*, *after*, or *during*. Others describe place, such as *over*, *in*, *on*, *above*, or *below*.

preposition

The runners raced <u>on</u> the track.

Thinking Question
What word shows a connection between other words in the sentence?

1–10. Find the preposition in each underlined phrase. Write the preposition on the line.

1. I read *Hercules the Mighty* long <u>into the night</u>. _____

2. Hercules had to fight <u>with many beasts and monsters</u>. _____

3. He had tremendous strength <u>in his muscles</u>. _____

4. <u>After my read-a-thon</u>, I dreamed I had super strength. _____

5. I could easily lift a house <u>over my head</u>. _____

6. My older brother stood <u>under the house</u> giving me orders. _____

7. When I awoke, he was <u>beside my bed</u> telling me to get up. _____

8. I have noticed my dreams <u>during the night</u> are often silly. _____

9. My brother does strength exercises <u>before school</u>. _____

10. Maybe that is why he was featured <u>in my crazy dream</u>. _____

Prepositional Phrases

A **prepositional phrase** begins with a preposition and ends with a noun or a pronoun. Both these words and all of the words in between them make up the prepositional phrase.

prepositional phrase

The girls have been best friends <u>for a long time</u>.

<u>At school</u>, they join many <u>of the same clubs</u>.

Thinking Question
What phrase begins with a preposition and ends with a noun or pronoun?

1–6. In each sentence below, underline the preposition. Write the prepositional phrase.

1. Myths say that Hercules once lived among ordinary humans.

   _____

2. Zeus watched Hercules from Mount Olympus.

   _____

3. Hercules completed impossible challenges on Earth.

   _____

4. Hercules only laughed at the dangerous tasks.

   _____

5. He showed that he was kind and helpful during his stay.

   _____

6. After his successes, Hercules could go home.

   _____

Prepositional Phrases to Provide Details

A prepositional phrase can also provide details to help describe a noun. The noun it helps describe is not part of the prepositional phrase.

noun described   **preposition**

Our school (play) this year is <u>about</u> a female athlete.

Thinking Questions
What is the prepositional phrase in the sentence? What details does it give about the sentence?

1–6. Look at the underlined preposition. Write a detail on the lines below to complete each sentence. Then circle the noun being described.

1. "Hercules' Quest" is a story about

   _____ .

2. It is a myth retold <u>by</u> _____ .

3. People <u>of</u> _____ enjoy myths

   and tales.

4. In Greek myths, Zeus rules from his kingdom <u>on</u>

   _____ .

5. We will be writing our own tales <u>for</u>

   _____ .

6. I will write a myth <u>about</u>

   _____ .

Sentence Fragments and Run-On Sentences

A sentence expresses a complete thought. It has a subject (the who or what) and a predicate (what the subject does or is). A sentence fragment lacks a subject or a predicate.

Complete sentence	Subject	Predicate
	The goddess Hera did not like baby Hercules.	
Sentence fragments	Many dangerous enemies. Lived in the kingdom.	
Run-on sentence	Hercules fought a lion, later he killed the hydra.	

To correct a sentence fragment, add the missing subject or predicate. One way to correct a run-on sentence is to put a period between the two sentences. Capitalize the first word in the second sentence.

1–5. Write *fragment* or *run-on* beside each group of words.
Correct the sentence error on the line. Use periods and capital letters correctly.

1. Had to gather golden apples for the king. _____

_____

2. A dragon guarded these apples it never slept. _____

_____

3. Hercules made a plan he would ask Atlas for help. _____

_____

4. tricked Atlas into getting the apples. _____

_____

5. The giant Atlas. _____

_____

Ideas

Use prepositional phrases to add interesting or important details to your writing.

> The hero fought the monster.
> The hero <u>with supernatural strength</u> fought the monster <u>with two heads</u>.

1–8 Add a prepositional phrase that provides descriptive detail to each sentence below.

1. The hero had to fight

_____.

2. A serpent was hiding

_____.

3. A lion frightened attackers

_____.

4. A dragon stood guard

_____.

5. The hero wanted to save the kingdom

_____.

6. The hero carried a sword

_____.

7. The hero's horse could fly

_____.

8. The hero's horse had wings

_____.

Focus Trait: Word Choice

You can vary your choice of descriptive words and details to make your writing more interesting.

Without Descriptive Words	With Descriptive Words
The hydra's heads turned toward Hercules.	The hydra's nine slimy heads spun around and bared their knife-sharp fangs at Hercules.

1–4 Rewrite the sentences to include descriptive adjectives, verbs, or phrases that add detail.

1. Hera was angry when Hercules killed the hydra.

_____

_____

2. The mountain of Atlas was huge.

_____

_____

3. Atlas grew tired and stiff from holding up the world.

_____

_____

4. As a boy, Hercules killed a lion.

_____

_____

Name _____ Date _____

Lesson 19
READER'S NOTEBOOK

Harvesting Hope: The
Story of Cesar Chavez
Independent Reading

Reader's Guide

Harvesting Hope:
The Story of Cesar Chavez

"Yes, It Can Be Done!"

Answer the questions below about Cesar Chavez's *La Causa*.
Then, draw a sign for *La Causa* on the next page.

Reread the third paragraph on page 566. What do you think the idiom "die of embarrassment" means? How does it help you understand how Cesar feels?

_____

_____

_____

Reread page 567. How did the members of *La Causa* choose to protest?

_____

_____

The Aztec eagle is a symbol of strength, patience, and courage. Why might Cesar have chosen a bold black eagle as the symbol for *La Causa?*

_____

_____

Design a sign that expresses the concerns and goals of *La Causa*. In your sign, include these ideas:

- a symbol for *La Causa* that relates to its goals, and
- a slogan that uses an idiom relating to *La Causa*.

Name _____ Date _____

Lesson 19
READER'S NOTEBOOK

**Harvesting Hope: The
Story of Cesar Chavez**
Vocabulary Strategies:
Reference Materials

Reference Materials

```
···················································
:    blur        strike      belief     :
:  suspicious    harvest     right      :
···················································
```

**Each sentence shows a word in *italics*. Use a dictionary to answer
questions about the words or to help you use them in a sentence.**

1. The word *blur* can be used as what parts of speech?

_____

2. How many syllables does the word *suspicious* have?

_____

3. Use the word *strike* with a different meaning in two sentences.

_____

_____

4. What guide words are found at the top of the page on which *harvest*
appears?

_____

5. According to your dictionary, which syllable of *belief* is the stressed
syllable? How can you tell?

_____

_____

6. Use the word *right* with a different meaning in two sentences.

_____

_____

Name _____ Date _____

Suffixes -ful, -less, -ness, -ment

Basic 1–11. Write the Basic Word that best fits each clue.

1. full of happiness _____

2. without end _____

3. a state of tidiness _____

4. concrete surface _____

5. unable to stay at rest _____

6. the act of moving _____

7. a state of having no strength _____

8. using more than is needed _____

9. sickness _____

10. having bright colors _____

11. affection _____

Challenge 12–15. Your school newspaper is featuring a health article. Your job is to submit some first-aid tips. Use four of the Challenge Words. Write on a separate sheet of paper.

Spelling Words

1. colorful
2. weakness
3. movement
4. endless
5. truthful
6. illness
7. cheerful
8. useless
9. beautiful
10. restless
11. clumsiness
12. pavement
13. peaceful
14. fondness
15. neatness
16. speechless
17. statement
18. wasteful
19. penniless
20. treatment

Challenge
numbness
ailment
resourceful
cleanliness
appointment

Spelling Word Sort

Harvesting Hope: The Story of Cesar Chavez
Spelling: Suffixes -ful, -less, -ness, -ment

Write each Basic Word beside the correct heading.

base word + -ful	**Basic Words:** **Challenge Words:** **Possible Selection Words:**
base word + -less	**Basic Words:**
base word + -ness	**Basic Words:** **Challenge Words:**
base word + -ment	**Basic Words:** **Challenge Words:** **Possible Selection Words:**

Challenge Add the Challenge Words to your Word Sort.

Connect to Reading Look through "Harvesting Hope: The Story of Cesar Chavez." Find words that have the suffixes *-ful*, *-less*, *-ness*, or *-ment*. Add them to your Word Sort.

Spelling Words

1. colorful
2. weakness
3. movement
4. endless
5. truthful
6. illness
7. cheerful
8. useless
9. beautiful
10. restless
11. clumsiness
12. pavement
13. peaceful
14. fondness
15. neatness
16. speechless
17. statement
18. wasteful
19. penniless
20. treatment

Challenge
numbness
ailment
resourceful
cleanliness
appointment

Proofreading for Spelling

Find the misspelled words and circle them. Write them correctly on the lines below.

Spelling Words

1. colorful
2. weakness
3. movement
4. endless
5. truthful
6. illness
7. cheerful
8. useless
9. beautiful
10. restless
11. clumsiness
12. pavement
13. peaceful
14. fondness
15. neatness
16. speechless
17. statement
18. wasteful
19. penniless
20. treatment

Challenge
numbness
ailment
resourceful
cleanliness
appointment

In 1948, Helen Fabela married Cesar Chavez, a man known for his endlest work to improve the treatmint of migrant farm workers in the United States. Though the couple endured rather peniles times and poor living conditions, Helen supported Cesar's work. She also made her own statment by starting a teaching program for Mexican farm workers.

Some dishonest people were not truthfil and started rumors about Mexican farm workers. Helen was spechles at the weekness of their values, and she thought it was uzeles to complain.

Helen had a chearful attitude, and she provided an environment for her husband and eight children that was beautyful and peaseful. Today Helen Chavez is an inspiration to her 31 grandchildren.

1. _____
2. _____
3. _____
4. _____
5. _____
6. _____
7. _____
8. _____
9. _____
10. _____
11. _____

Clauses

A **clause** is a group of words with a subject and predicate. If a clause can stand alone as a sentence, it is an **independent clause**. A **dependent clause** cannot stand alone. Many dependent clauses begin with a transition word such as *before, after, since, because, who, whose, that,* or *which.*

Dependent Clause   Independent Clause
Since they had no water for crops, they had to leave the ranch.

Independent Clause   Dependent Clause
Chavez was the leader that the workers chose.

Thinking Questions
What clauses can stand alone? Which clauses cannot stand alone?

1–6.   Underline the dependent clause in each sentence. Circle the transition word that introduces the dependent clause.

1. After they worked long hours, migrant workers had little to eat.

2. Workers who complained to the owners were fired, punished, or even killed.

3. The farm workers suffered because their work was so hard.

4. Until Chavez organized the workers, they had no way to fight back.

5. After the workers began to march, other people learned about their cause.

6. A huge, cheering crowd met the marchers when they reached Sacramento.

Relative Pronouns

Some dependent clauses begin with a relative pronoun, such as *who, whom, whose, that,* or *which.* These clauses act as adjectives and answer the questions *Which one?* or *What kind?* about a noun or pronoun.

Dependent Clause: California is the state **that** produces the most fruit crops. [tells which state]

Dependent Clause: This farm, **which** grows strawberries, is the largest in the state. [tells what kind of farm]

Thinking Question
Which word introduces a dependent clause that tells about the noun that comes before if?

1–5. Circle the relative pronoun in each sentence. Underline the dependent clause. Write the noun or pronoun this clause describes on the line at the right.

1. There was a terrible drought that caused the Chavez family to lose their ranch. _____

2. They moved to California, which offered jobs for migrant farm workers. _____

3. A worker whose job is so harsh may complain. _____

4. Migrant children, who move often, have difficulty keeping up in school. _____

5. The strike, which the grape company opposed, was finally a success. _____

Lesson 19
READER'S NOTEBOOK

**Harvesting Hope: The
Story of Cesar Chavez**
Grammar: Relative Pronouns
and Adverbs

Relative Adverbs in Clauses

Relative adverbs begin dependent clauses that tell
where, when or *why*.

Thinking Question
*Which word introduces a
dependent clause that tells
about a place, a time, or a
reason?*

Dependent Clause

I can tell you **why** migrant workers loved Cesar
Chavez.
California is the place **where** La Causa was born.
Do you know **when** Chavez was born?

1–6.   **Underline the dependent clause in each sentence. Circle
the relative adverb that begins the clause.**

1. That Arizona ranch is where Chavez lived as a young boy.

2. The family had to move away when a drought ruined the
   crops.

3. Their sad mother told them why they had to leave their
   home.

4. The family had to live in a dirty shed when they arrived in
   California.

5. I wonder why the landowner treated workers so poorly.

6. An old theater in Fresno is where the first National Farm
   Workers meeting took place.

Prepositions and Prepositional Phrases

Prepositions	Prepositional Phrases
from, to	The farm workers walked from Delano to Sacramento.

1–5. Underline the preposition twice and the rest of the prepositional phrase once in each sentence.

1. Most farms in the valley are large.

2. Many farms use modern equipment for plowing, planting, and harvesting.

3. However, tender fruit crops are harvested by hand.

4. Farm workers bend, pull, and sweat under the hot sun.

5. After a long day, they are ready to rest and enjoy themselves.

6–7. Combine each set of sentences, using prepositional phrases correctly. Write the new sentence on the line.

6. Our family is proud. We are proud of our good work.

_____

_____

7. Chavez was proud but humble. He was proud of his heritage. He felt humble about his achievements.

_____

_____

Sentence Fluency

> Transition words help writers combine ideas. They show readers how ideas and events are related.

1–6. Complete the sentences below by writing transition words from the box.

> as a result   however   since
> in short   because   finally

1. Many people lost their farms _____ a terrible drought occurred.

2. _____, there was work available on the rich farms in California.

3. _____, they became migrant workers for large California farms.

4. _____ their pay was so low, they couldn't afford decent housing.

5. _____, they formed *La Causa* to fight against harsh conditions and low wages.

6. _____, their goals were to increase wages and improve working conditions.

Focus Trait: Organization
Planning a Personal Narrative

A personal narrative is a story about something that happened in your life.

A. For your personal narrative, choose an event that you remember well or that has special meaning to you. Then fill in the blanks below to help you plan your story.

Topic: I will write about _____

What happened first: _____

Next: _____

Last: _____

What I learned: _____

B. Think about how the ideas in your narrative are connected. Write transition words to show time or place, cause and effect, and how or what kind.

Pair/Share Work with a partner to brainstorm sample sentences with two clauses. Underline the transition words you use.

_____

_____

_____

_____

_____

Name _____ Date _____

Lesson 20
READER'S NOTEBOOK

Sacagawea
Independent Reading

 Reader's Guide

Sacagawea

Sacagawea's Journal

Review the events of Sacagawea's time with Lewis and Clark during the summer of 1805. Answer the questions below to help write a journal entry by Sacagawea.

Reread pages 592–593. When the boat carrying their supplies tipped, how was Sacagawea's reaction different from her husband's? What does this tell you about Sacagawea?

_____

_____

Reread pages 594–595. Why was traveling so difficult for Sacagawea and the explorers in June and July of 1805?

_____

_____

List two details that tell the difficulties Sacagawea and the explorers faced during the summer of 1805.

_____

_____

What did Sacagawea do when she saw her people, the Shoshone? How does this compare with the way she acted until this point?

_____

_____

Independent Reading
241
Grade 4, Unit 4

Write Sacagawea's journal entry retelling the events of the
summer of 1805. In the journal entry, infer what Sacagawea
may have been feeling while she was traveling with Lewis and Clark
using the details you found.

Shades of Meaning

Synonyms are words that have similar meanings. They do not mean exactly the same thing. Synonyms may give us different feelings about the subject. For example, if a boat is **winding** upstream, it is traveling that way somewhat slowly. However, if the boat is **wandering** upstream, the journey is even slower and less direct.

Circle the synonym that best fits the context for each sentence. On the line, write why you chose this word.

1. I love to read about explorers and imagine I'm along on their (wild, crazy) adventures.

   _____

   _____

2. Sacagawea made the (bold, brash) decision to join the Corps of Discovery.

   _____

   _____

3. The crew had not eaten for days and (yearned, wished) for a meal.

   _____

   _____

4. The Corps would never have made it to the Pacific without their (strong-willed, pig-headed) leaders.

   _____

   _____

5. Sacagawea became (important, invaluable) to the mission.

   _____

   _____

Words with VCCV Pattern

Basic 1–10.   Write the Basic Word that completes each analogy.

1. *Happily* is to *joyously* as *rarely* is to _____ .

2. *Shoe* is to *sneaker* as *spice* is to _____ .

3. *Omelet* is to *eggs* as *house* is to _____ .

4. *Give* is to *receive* as *lend* is to _____ .

5. *Puddle* is to *ocean* as *dollar* is to _____ .

6. *Quarterback* is to *football* as *goalie* is to
   _____ .

7. *Carpenter* is to *house* as *photographer* is to
   _____ .

8. *Mountain* is to *peak* as *ravine* is to _____ .

9. *Dentist* is to *teeth* as *mechanic* is to _____ .

10. *Safety* is to *security* as *peril* is to _____ .

Challenge 11–14.   Write an e-mail to a friend about a movie you
have seen recently. Describe a scene that you liked. Use four
Challenge Words. Write on a separate sheet of paper.

Spelling Words

1. million
2. collect
3. lumber
4. pepper
5. plastic
6. borrow
7. support
8. thirty
9. perfect
10. attend
11. canyon
12. traffic
13. fortune
14. danger
15. soccer
16. engine
17. picture
18. survive
19. seldom
20. effort

Challenge
occur
venture
challenge
rascal
splendid

Name _____ Date _____

Spelling Word Sort

Write each Basic Word beside the correct heading.

		Spelling Words
VCCV Pattern: Double consonants	Basic Words:	1. million
		2. collect
		3. lumber
	Challenge Words:	4. pepper
		5. plastic
		6. borrow
	Possible Selection Words:	7. support
		8. thirty
	Basic Words:	9. perfect
		10. attend
VCCV Pattern: Different consonants		11. canyon
		12. traffic
		13. fortune
	Challenge Words:	14. danger
		15. soccer
		16. engine
	Possible Selection Words:	17. picture
		18. survive
		19. seldom
		20. effort

Challenge   Add the Challenge Words to your Word Sort.

Connect to Reading   Look through "Sacagawea." Find words that have the VCCV pattern. Add them to your Word Sort.

Challenge
occur
venture
challenge
rascal
splendid

Proofreading for Spelling

Sacagawea
Spelling: Words with
VCCV Pattern

Find the misspelled words and circle them. Write them correctly on the lines below.

On their trip west, Lewis and Clark hired a French trader for his knowledge of Indian languages. Then they discovered that the trader's wife, Sacagawea, gave the crew more language suport than the trader. She was perfec for the job. Sacagawea would atend meetings between the explorers and Indians to be the interpreter. Even though the group did not meet much trafic on the trail, Sacagawea did not have time to be lonely. She would walk down the canyonn to colleck any food she could find for the more than thirte men to eat. When Sacagawea found a bush with what seemed like a milion berries on it, she couldn't pickure a better forchun. Her extra effert helped the crew servive the long journey. Lewis and Clark owed a lot to Sacagawea.

1. _____

2. _____

3. _____

4. _____

5. _____

6. _____

7. _____

8. _____

9. _____

10. _____

11. _____

12. _____

Spelling Words

1. million
2. collect
3. lumber
4. pepper
5. plastic
6. borrow
7. support
8. thirty
9. perfect
10. attend
11. canyon
12. traffic
13. fortune
14. danger
15. soccer
16. engine
17. picture
18. survive
19. seldom
20. effort

Challenge
occur
venture
challenge
rascal
splendid

Name _____ Date _____

Abbreviations for People and Places

An **abbreviation** is a short form of a word. Most abbreviations begin with a capital letter and end with a period. Both letters of state name abbreviations are capital letters, and no period is used.

Person	Mr. Hideki Nomo
Place	55 Porter Blvd.
Place	Shoreline, WA 98155

Thinking Question
What parts of the address are shortened forms of words?

1–8. Write each group of words. Use an abbreviation for the underlined word or words.

1. Shoshone Trading <u>Company</u> _____

2. Charles Pompy, <u>Junior</u> _____

3. 92 Mountain <u>Road</u> _____

4. <u>Doctor</u> May Dawson _____

5. 195 Water <u>Street</u> _____

6. <u>Mister</u> Robert Woods, <u>Senior</u> _____

7. 16 Muddy Creek <u>Drive</u> _____

8. Beavercreek, <u>Oregon</u> 97004 _____

Abbreviations for Mailing Addresses

An **abbreviation** is a short form of a word. Use abbreviations when writing street names and states in a mailing address. Abbreviate words such as *road* or *avenue* with a capital letter and end with a period. Write both letters of state name abbreviations with capital letters and do not use periods.

Thinking Questions
What parts of an address can I make shorter? How can I shorten the whole word?

Road	Rd.	Court	Ct.
Street	St.	Post Office	P.O.
Avenue	Ave.	Boulevard	Blvd.

Write each mailing address using abbreviations.

Full Address	Abbreviated Address
1. Mister Pedro Saravia The Total Pet Supply Company 9302 Riverside Drive Toledo, Ohio 43601	
2. Miss Alexis Parker The Press Building 14 Paper Lane Seattle, Washington 98104	
3. Gregory Nulman President, Choice Restaurants Post Office Box 269 Brooklyn, New York 11216	

Abbreviations for Time and Measurement

An **abbreviation** is a short form of a word. The abbreviations for days and months begin with a capital letter and end with a period. Some other abbreviations for time and measurements begin with a lowercase letter and end with a period.

Thinking Questions
What parts can I make shorter? How can I shorten the whole word?

time	measurement
Wed., Aug. 26	165 mi., 4 yd.

1–10. Write these groups of words, using correct abbreviations.

1. 8,000 feet _____

2. 1 hour, 45 minutes _____

3. Tuesday, January 7, 1806 _____

4. Monday–Friday _____

5. 3 yards, 11 inches _____

6. April 30, 1803 _____

7. November 24, 2014 _____

8. Thursday, February 27, 1805 _____

9. 7 hours, 15 minutes _____

10. March 10, 1922 _____

Frequently Confused Words

These words sound the same, but their meanings and spellings are different.

ate/eight	The hungry men caught **eight** fish and **ate** every one for supper.
core/corps	Expert craftsmen were the **core** of the **Corps** of Discovery.
horse/hoarse	A tired man spoke in a **hoarse** voice about the **horse** he had lost.
meat/meet	When they would **meet** with Shoshone leaders, they would feast on **meat.**
their/there	**Their** goal was to reach the Pacific Ocean and return home from **there.**
threw/through	Traveling **through** the wilderness, they **threw** nothing useful away.

1–8.   Circle the correct word in parentheses ( ).

1. Lewis and Clark's (core, corps) of men was united by a vital, exciting mission.

2. Since they set out traveling on a keelboat, the men had not a single (hoarse, horse) with them.

3. (Their, There) 55-foot boat carried 12 tons of supplies and gifts to give the Shoshone.

4. They would hunt for the (meat, meet) to feed the crew as they traveled.

5. In the mountain passage, the explorers (ate, eight) very little. In fact, they almost starved.

6. For over two years, the group traveled (threw, through) American wilderness.

7. The success and discoveries of the expedition (threw, through) Americans into a fever of excitement.

8. Sacagawea never dreamed she would (meat, meet) her brother, who had become a Shoshone chief.

Name _____ Date _____

Lesson 20
READER'S NOTEBOOK

Sacagawea
Grammar: Connect to Writing

Conventions

Each group of words has two incorrect abbreviations. Use proofreading marks to correct the abbreviations.

1. Mr. and mrs Tom Charbonneau, Jr.

1804 Hidatsa Dr.

Sioux City, Ia., 51101

2. Frid., Febr'y. 14

3. 55 mls per hour on the Fort Mandan expy

4. mond., octob 22

5. Doc. Michelle Mitchell

431 Expedition boulv'd

Bethel, ME 04217

6. 17 In, 3 ft., 4 yrd.

Focus Trait: Ideas
Choosing Interesting, Important Details

Good writers try to use details that will interest the reader. The details should connect to the main events of the narrative.

With Dull, Unimportant Details	With Interesting, Important Details
Newborn Jean-Baptiste Charbonneau began life with a grand adventure. **He became a favorite of William Clark. (not important)** Carried on his mother's back, the infant rode the whitewater of rivers. **He saw a lot of wildlife. (dull)**	Newborn Jean-Baptiste Charbonneau began life with a grand adventure. Carried on his mother's back, the infant rode the whitewater of rivers. He saw buffalo, wolves, bighorn sheep, and fierce grizzly bears.

Read the sets of sentences. Cross out details that are dull or not important. Then rewrite the sentences on the lines.

1. Jean-Baptiste became very ill in 1806 on the return journey. He had a fever. His neck and throat swelled up. A mixture of bear oil, pine resin, and wild onions helped him recover. The boy went on to have an interesting life.

_____

_____

_____

_____

Rewrite the next sentences on a separate sheet of paper. Replace the underlined words with more interesting, important details.

2. It would be cool to have an adventure like Jean-Baptiste. Tomorrow's child might be born on the moon or journey to Mars. It might be dangerous. It would always be interesting.

Reader's Guide

Horses

A Horse and a Human

Horses and humans have a unique history.
In each square, draw and label a horse and rider
in history. Use what you read on pages 2–3 to help you.
Leave one square to draw yourself and horses.

Name _____ Date _____

Unit 4
READER'S NOTEBOOK

Horses
Segment 1
Independent Reading

A Horse History

Read page 4. Use what you have read to make a timeline to describe horses and their ancestors.

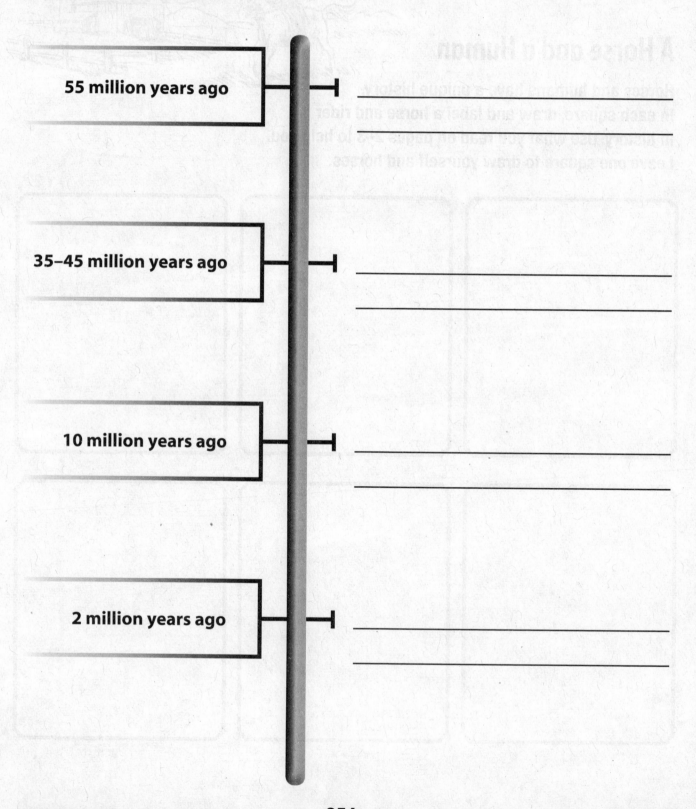

55 million years ago

35–45 million years ago

10 million years ago

2 million years ago

What Big Teeth You Have!

Horses have changed a lot in 55 million years.
One change has been what they eat.

Read pages 4–5, and then imagine that you are a scientist studying the changes of horses over time. In your own words, write a summary of horses, their diets, and their teeth.

_____

_____

_____

_____

_____

_____

_____

_____

_____

_____

_____

_____

_____

_____

Name _____ Date _____

Besides grasses, horses today eat other things.
Now imagine that you are in charge of the diets of
the horses at Blue Ridge Farms. What will you serve?

**Read pages 5–9. Design a menu for the horses. Think about
menus you have seen and use your imagination to create a
fun menu for the farm. Illustrate your menu.**

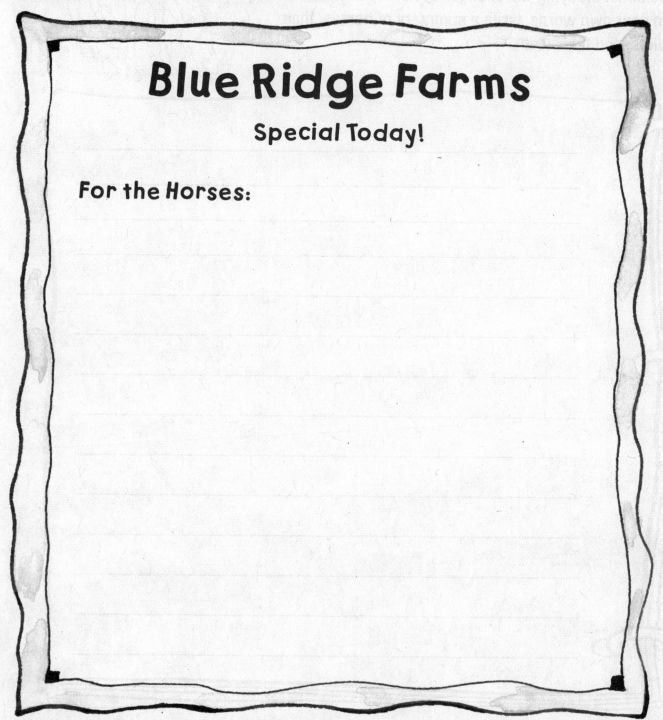

Blue Ridge Farms
Special Today!

For the Horses:

Alike and Different

Horses and people have the same senses, but they do not work the same way. Read page 9. For each sense, create a diagram to show the differences and similarities between horse senses and human senses. Label your diagram with information from the book.

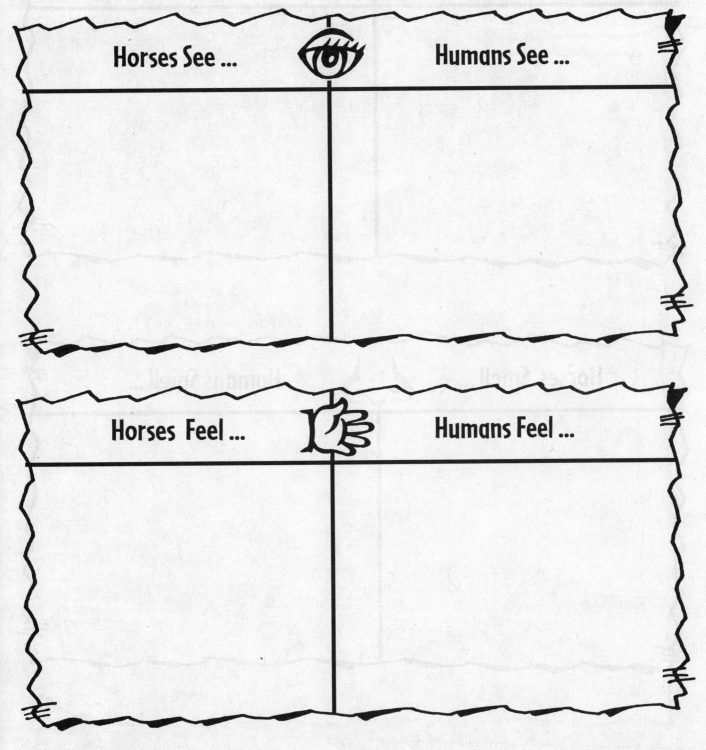

Horses See ...   Humans See ...

Horses Feel ...   Humans Feel ...

Name _____ Date _____

Unit 4
READER'S NOTEBOOK

Horses
Segment 1
Independent Reading

Horses Hear ...   Humans Hear ...

Horses Smell ...   Humans Smell ...

Name _____ Date _____

Unit 4
READER'S NOTEBOOK

Horses
Segment 2
Independent Reading

Reader's Guide

Horses

A Horse Family

You have read about the different names horses have that describe their age and whether they are male or female. Design a horse photo album. In each square, draw a portrait of a horse. Then label each portrait with a name. Describe what each name means. Use the names you read on page 11.

Communication

Horses cannot talk like humans, but they can communicate. Use what you have read on page 12. In the left column, describe three things you might see horses do. In the middle column, describe what it means. In the right column, explain what you might do if you saw a horse trying to communicate.

What Horses Do	What It Means	What You Can Do

Name _____ Date _____

Unit 4
READER'S NOTEBOOK

Horses
Segment 2
Independent Reading

Move Like a Horse

Horses walk, cantor, trot, and gallop. Read page 15.
In each box, draw a horse in a different gait. Begin with
the fastest gait and end with the slowest gait. Explain in your
own words how people can identify at what speed a horse is moving.

_____

_____

_____

_____

Name _____ Date _____

Unit 4
READER'S NOTEBOOK

Horses
Segment 2
Independent Reading

Name _____ Date _____

Unit 4
READER'S NOTEBOOK

Horses
Segment 2
Independent Reading

Horses in the Zoo

You have learned many different things about horses. As a horse expert, a zoo has called you to make a plaque to inform visitors about the horses.

Think about the most important information you have read through page 15. Think about interesting information zoo visitors might want to read. Create a plaque to tell about horses.

A New Baby in the Zoo

When babies are born in the zoo, the zookeepers often send announcements to local newspapers. Write a press release for a new baby horse! Do not forget to give the baby a unique name.

❧ Press Release ❧

Name:

_____

Date of birth:

_____

_____

Will I be a filly or a colt? Why?

_____

_____

_____

How can you tell which mare is my mother?

_____

_____

_____

_____

Name _____ Date _____

Unit 4
READER'S NOTEBOOK

Horses
Segment 3
Independent Reading

 Reader's Guide

Horses

A Picture Dictionary

There are many names for the colors of horses. Use what you have read to create a picture dictionary to show the differences between the words.

Read pages 16–17. Use crayons or colored pencils to color the horses according to their names.

Bay   **Palomino**

Name _____ Date _____

Unit 4
READER'S NOTEBOOK

Horses
Segment 3
Independent Reading

Dun   Skewbald

The names for horse colors may be hard to remember.
Think of a trick that can help you remember the meaning
of one of the color names and write it below.

_____

_____

_____

_____

Name _____ Date _____

Horse Riddles

In this book about horses, there are many new words. Read the following riddles and see if you can figure out what new word the riddle describes. If you need a hint, read the page shown under the riddle.

I am an ancestor of the modern horse. I was the size of a large dog. I ate grasses and leaves.

Which ancestor am I?

_____

_____

_____

Need a clue? Read page 4.

I am the word that describes the way horses move. If you spell me differently, I mean an opening in a wall or fence.

What word am I?

_____

_____

_____

Need a clue? Read page 15.

I am a word to describe the color of many horses. If I am light, I am called dun. If I am dark, I am called chestnut.

What color am I?

_____

_____

_____

Need a clue? Read page 16.

I am a word to describe the color of a horse. I am the word to describe a horse that is black and white.

What color word am I?

_____

_____

Need a clue? Read page 17.

Name _____ Date _____

Write two riddles about words you have learned about horses. Give your readers clues to solve the riddles using what you have read. Write the page from *Horses,* where your reader can find more clues if he or she needs some.

Now turn your paper upside down.
Write the answers to your riddles on this line.

_____

Name _____   Date _____

Horses: Hotbloods, Coldbloods, Warmbloods

In this section, you have read about the three groups of horse breeds. Use what you learned to take notes. Then follow the directions to write an online encyclopedia article.

First, take notes on the three types of horse breeds. Reread pages 19–23 to review the similarities and differences. Include examples of each type, where each type lives, and how humans use each type.

Name _____ Date _____

Unit 4
READER'S NOTEBOOK

Horses
Segment 3
Independent Reading

Now use your notes to create an online encyclopedia article. Remember to include headings. After each heading, include specific examples and details of each breed.

File   Edit   View   Favorites   Tools   Help

Address ⓔ

Go

Horse Breeds

Heading 1: _____

_____

_____

_____

Heading 2: _____

_____

_____

_____

Heading 3: _____

_____

_____

_____

ⓔ   🌐 Internet

Name _____ Date _____

Unit 4
READER'S NOTEBOOK

Horses
Segment 4
Independent Reading

Horses

Pony Wanted

You would like to buy a pony. Think about why a person might need a pony and then write a want ad for a newspaper. How will you take care of the pony? What makes you the best owner for this pony? Use persuasive words to convince the person to sell you the pony. Read pages 24–25 for more information.

WANTED: PONY

_____

_____

_____

_____

_____

_____

_____

_____

_____

_____

Name _____   Date _____

Unit 4
READER'S NOTEBOOK

Horses
Segment 4
Independent Reading

Be a Photojournalist

Look at the photographs throughout *Horses*. You should notice that some of the pictures show how strong workhorses are. Others show off the beautiful colors. The photos on pages 26–27 show the wildness of feral mustangs. Imagine that you want photos of the feral ponies in Britain. Write a note describing the type of photo that you would want to show off the ponies' unique qualities. Be sure to note what the background should look like and what the photo should show the ponies doing.

Assignment: Feral Ponies of Britain

Notes:

Name _____ Date _____

Today and Yesterday

In *Horses*, you have read many different ways in which humans have used horses. Some of these examples are from the present. Some of these examples are from the past.

Draw and label three ways people used horses years ago.

Name _____ Date _____

Unit 4
READER'S NOTEBOOK

Horses
Segment 4
Independent Reading

Draw and label ways people use horses today.

Name _____ Date _____

Unit 4
READER'S NOTEBOOK

Horses
Segment 4
Independent Reading

Dear Editor

Look at the drawings you created about horses and people yesterday and today on pages 273–274. Pretend that you visited a farm that used horses. Write a letter to the editor of your school newspaper about your experience. Explain why you think the school should go to this farm for a field trip.

Dear Editor,

_____

_____

_____

_____

_____

_____

_____

_____

_____

_____

Sincerely,

_____

My Library

Write a review of *Horses*. Fill in from one to five stars to rate the book. Explain one thing you learned that was interesting. Then explain what you thought of the book. Use examples from the book to support the ideas in your review.

Horses

I rate this book: ☆ ☆ ☆ ☆ ☆

_____

_____

_____

_____

_____

_____

_____

_____

_____

Reader's Guide

The World According to Humphrey

A. J.'s Proposal

A. J. may have learned more than what it is like to take care of a hamster for a weekend. Imagine that A. J. wants to tell what he learned about the harmful effects of watching too much television. Write a proposal in which A. J. tells his classmates why they should have a "Weekly TV-Free Night." First, answer the questions below.

Reread pages 628 and 632–633. How have A. J.'s nighttime activities changed?

_____

_____

_____

Look at the illustrations on pages 628 and 633. How does the family look in each illustration?

_____

_____

_____

How can too much television affect a family?

_____

_____

_____

Name _____   Date _____

Lesson 21
READER'S NOTEBOOK

The World According
to Humphrey
Independent Reading

Write A. J.'s proposal for a "Weekly TV-Free Night" to his
fellow classmates. What might A. J. say about watching too
much television based on what happened over the weekend?
Give A. J.'s argument about why it would be good for everyone to
turn off the television at least one night a week. Use details from
the story to support A. J.'s argument.

I Propose a Weekly TV-Free Night

_____

_____

_____

_____

_____

_____

_____

_____

_____

Using Context

```
figure      might        cover       racket
block       corner       pet         combination
```

**Each sentence below contains a multiple-meaning word. Read
each sentence. Fill in the circle next to the definition that fits the
way the word is used in the sentence.**

1. Alma was able to <u>figure</u> out a hard math problem.
   - ○ **A.** understand
   - ○ **B.** a shape

2. The two friends lived on the same <u>block</u>.
   - ○ **A.** get in the way of
   - ○ **B.** a section of a street

3. He used all his <u>might</u> to pick up the heavy box.
   - ○ **A.** maybe
   - ○ **B.** strength

4. I will put my desk in the <u>corner</u> of the room.
   - ○ **A.** place where two walls meet
   - ○ **B.** to trap

5. The music was a <u>combination</u> of rock and jazz styles.
   - ○ **A.** numbers used to open a lock
   - ○ **B.** a mix or blend of things

6. You should <u>cover</u> your head with a hat when it is cold.
   - ○ **A.** a blanket
   - ○ **B.** to put something on top of
     something else

7. My friend asked if he could <u>pet</u> my dog.
   - ○ **A.** stroke an animal
   - ○ **B.** an animal kept by humans

8. I left my <u>racket</u> at a friend's house.
   - ○ **A.** something used to play tennis
   - ○ **B.** a loud noise

Words with VCV Pattern

Basic 1–10. Read the paragraph. Write the Basic Word that best replaces the underlined word or words in each sentence.

Moving to a new place was an (1) <u>important occasion</u> in my life. I was only a (2) <u>person who studies</u> when my family shot into space. We flew to the (3) <u>heavenly body</u> Zondora. The shuttle flight from Earth to Zondora was very (4) <u>fast</u>. We stayed in a hovering (5) <u>resort</u>. The workers there were (6) <u>respectful</u> and helpful. Zondora has large lava pits and (7) <u>icy</u> plains. It has a large shield to (8) <u>protect</u> against anything that could harm the planet. If the shield is threatened, a (9) <u>device that makes a loud noise</u> blares. The people (10) <u>join together</u> to keep Zondora safe.

1. _____	6. _____
2. _____	7. _____
3. _____	8. _____
4. _____	9. _____
5. _____	10. _____

Spelling Words

1. event
2. humor
3. rapid
4. music
5. relief
6. planet
7. detail
8. unite
9. frozen
10. figure
11. siren
12. polite
13. hotel
14. protest
15. punish
16. defend
17. relay
18. habit
19. student
20. moment

Challenge
rumor
jealous
license
image
rival

Challenge 11–14. Your brother and your best friend are on opposing teams of a football game. Write a journal entry that tells how you cheered for both teams. Use four of the Challenge Words. Write on a separate sheet of paper.

Spelling Word Sort

The World According to Humphrey
Spelling: Words with VCV Pattern

Write each Basic Word beside the correct heading.

VC/V: Divide after the consonant	**Basic Words:**
	Challenge Words:
	Possible Selection Words:
V/CV: Divide before the consonant	**Basic Words:**
	Challenge Words:
	Possible Selection Words:

Challenge   Add the Challenge Words to your Word Sort.

Connect to Reading   Look through "The World According to Humphrey." Find words that have the VC / V and V / CV spelling pattern on this page. Add them to your Word Sort.

Spelling Words

1. event
2. humor
3. rapid
4. music
5. relief
6. planet
7. detail
8. unite
9. frozen
10. figure
11. siren
12. polite
13. hotel
14. protest
15. punish
16. defend
17. relay
18. habit
19. student
20. moment

Challenge
rumor
jealous
license
image
rival

Name _____ Date _____

Proofreading for Spelling

Find the misspelled words and circle them. Write them correctly on the lines below.

What a releef to be back at school! If only I could talk, I would ask Mrs. Brisbane for a momint of her time to protes the weekend's arrangement at the Thomases' house. Don't get me wrong now. The family treated me nicely, and they did not punich me when water spilled inside my cage. They actually thought it was an exciting ivent! Mr. Thomas thinks he has a great sense of humer, but here's a small deteil that I'll only share with Mrs. Brisbane: his jokes are the corniest on the planit. Mrs. Thomas is very pollite, but her taste in muzic is simply awful. She also has a very bad habet of serving frozin pizza that isn't cooked through. "Look at our little hamster go!" Mrs. Brisbane said. "He's running a relae race on his wheel. I think he's glad to be back."

Spelling Words

1. event
2. humor
3. rapid
4. music
5. relief
6. planet
7. detail
8. unite
9. frozen
10. figure
11. siren
12. polite
13. hotel
14. protest
15. punish
16. defend
17. relay
18. habit
19. student
20. moment

Challenge
rumor
jealous
license
image
rival

1. _____
2. _____
3. _____
4. _____
5. _____
6. _____
7. _____
8. _____
9. _____
10. _____
11. _____
12. _____
13. _____

Name _____ Date _____

Comparative Forms of Adjectives

A **comparative adjective** compares one person, place, or thing to another. To form a comparative adjective, you can usually add *-er* to the adjective. If the adjective ends in *y*, change the *y* to *i* before adding *-er*.

Thinking Questions
Are there two persons, places, or things being compared? Does the adjective end in -er or use more?

adjective

Josh is <u>tall</u>.
The weather is <u>dry</u> today.

comparative adjective

Jacob is <u>taller</u> than Josh.
The weather is <u>drier</u> today than yesterday.

1–4. Write the comparative form of the adjective in each sentence.

1. I think that spring feels (warm) _____ than winter.
2. My dog seems hungry, but your dog looks _____ .
3. Maddie is short, but Cindy is _____ .
4. Her song is lovely, but I think your song sounds _____ .

Some comparative adjectives are formed by adding the word *more*. Usually longer adjectives form the comparative this way.

Joe is <u>more polite</u> than Henry.

5–8. Write the comparative form of each adjective.

5. Sally felt (miserable) _____ when she knew she had the flu.
6. That company is (efficient) _____ than its competitor.
7. Will you feel (comfortable) _____ sitting here?
8. Tonight's dinner tastes (delicious) _____ than last night's.

Superlative Forms of Adjectives

When we use adjectives to compare more than two persons, places, or things, we use the superlative form of the adjective. To form a **superlative adjective**, add -*est* or write *most* before the adjective.

Thinking Questions
Are there more than two persons, places, or things being compared? Does the adjective end in -est or use most*?*

Adjective	Comparative	Superlative
happy	happier	happiest
complex	more complex	most complex

Emily is <u>luckier</u> than Mary, but Alyssa is the <u>luckiest</u> of all.

Without a map, Gregory is <u>more confused</u> than Lew, but Edwin is the <u>most confused</u>.

1–5. Write the correct form of the adjective in parentheses to complete the sentence.

1. A rose is pretty, but Tom thinks an orchid is (pretty)

   _____.

2. Susan says that of all the flowers, the peony is the (pretty)

   _____.

3. This tulip is the (bright) _____ shade of red I've

   ever seen.

4. Carrie told him that lavender smells (wonderful)

   _____.

5. Trees grow the (tall) _____ of all plants.

Comparative and Superlative Forms of Adverbs

Adverbs often work with verbs and tell how, when, or where an action happens. They are used with action verbs, and many end with *-ly*. A **comparative adverb** compares the action of two or more things. The word *more* is often used. A **superlative adverb** compares the action of more than two things. The word *most* is often used.

Adverb	Comparative	Superlative
slowly	more slowly	most slowly
soon	sooner	soonest
promptly	more promptly	most promptly

Thinking Questions
Does the adverb end in -ly? Is the word more *or* most *added?*

Use a comparative or superlative adverb for each blank below. Use the list on the right to help you complete the sentences.

1. Although many musicians were loud, Donald played the trumpet _____.

2. Sarah could add numbers _____ than her brother.

3. Jerry ran _____ than his best friend.

4. Of all my friends, Carmin lives _____.

5. Marty worked _____ on the project than his partner.

6. Jeremy answered the question _____ of the three contestants.

louder
loudest
more quickly
most quickly
more completely
most completely
closer
closest
harder
hardest
faster
fastest

Prepositions and Prepositional Phrases

Preposition	Prepositional Phrase
from	Removing a wild animal *from* its home is not wise.

Underline the preposition twice and the rest of the prepositional phrase once in each sentence.

1. The young turtles stepped slowly into the busy, dangerous road.

2. Ms. Roland spotted the three turtles on her long walk.

3. She treats all animals with respect and kindness.

4. She carried the young turtles to safety.

5. The tiny creatures had wandered from the green, grassy marsh.

6. The marsh beside the forest was a better home than the highway!

Combine each pair of sentences. Write the new sentence on the line. Capitalize and punctuate correctly.

7. Ms. Roland hummed as she walked. She walked to her home.

_____

8. She fed her fish and watched them. They swam around their tank.

_____

9. You should be happy. You should be happy you live in a safe home.

_____

Word Choice

Using more exact comparative and superlative adjectives and
adverbs can make your writing more interesting.

Less Exact	More Exact
Dinner smells <u>better</u> than lunch.	Dinner smells <u>spicier</u> and <u>more delicious</u> than lunch.
The big box is the <u>heaviest</u>.	The big box is the <u>most impossible</u> to fit!

**Rewrite each sentence to make it more interesting. Try to use
more exact adjectives and adverbs.**

1. My favorite star is brighter than a light bulb.

    _____

2. It is maybe the brightest star.

    _____

3. Don't you think the sun shines more clearly than
   your star?

    _____

4. The sun seems so strong to us because it is the closest to us.

    _____

5. The sun's role in our lives is bigger than the moon's.

    _____

6. Sun energy is even better than wind energy.

    _____

Name _____ Date _____

Lesson 21
READER'S NOTEBOOK

The World According
to Humphrey
Writing: Informative Writing

Focus Trait: Ideas

> You can make your ideas clearer if your paragraph has a topic sentence. Remove unimportant or unnecessary details to help support the main idea better.

Read the paragraph below. Circle the sentence that would make the best topic sentence to start the paragraph. Underline two details that do not belong in the paragraph.

One of the earliest toothbrushes was called the "chew stick." It was made from a twig about the size of a pencil. One end of the twig was pointed. The other end was chewed until it became soft and brushlike. People brushed with the chewed end. They cleaned between their teeth with the pointed end. New Orleans dentist Levi Spear Parmly (1790–1859) is credited as the inventor of modern dental floss. You might be surprised to learn that people have been using toothbrushes for thousands and thousands of years. The Chinese were the first to make and use toothbrushes with bristles. The handle was carved from bone or bamboo. The bristles were made from animal hair and then attached to one end of the handle. These stiff bristles did a better job cleaning teeth than the chew stick. The first nylon toothbrush was called Doctor West's Miracle Toothbrush.

Name _____ Date _____

Lesson 22
READER'S NOTEBOOK

I Could Do That!
Esther Morris Gets
Women the Vote
Independent Reading

Reader's Guide

I Could Do That!
Esther Morris Gets
Women the Vote

Interview with Mrs. Esther Morris

A reporter has come to interview Mrs. Esther Morris, the first woman to hold public office in America. Help complete the interview by answering the questions below.

> Esther, your mother died when you were very young. What effect did your mother's death have on you?

Reread page 657 to give Esther's answer.

_____

_____

> Why did you start your own business at such a young age?

Reread the first paragraph of page 658 to give Esther's answer.

_____

_____

Name _____ Date _____

Lesson 22
READER'S NOTEBOOK

I Could Do That!
Esther Morris Gets
Women the Vote
Independent Reading

After your husband's death, you moved to Illinois to reclaim his land. The law kept you from owning the land because you were a woman. What effect did this have on you?

Reread page 659. What effect might this have had on Esther? Use these answers to give Esther's response.

_____

_____

Why do you think it is important for women to have the same rights as men?

Think of Esther's character and the events of her life to help write her response.

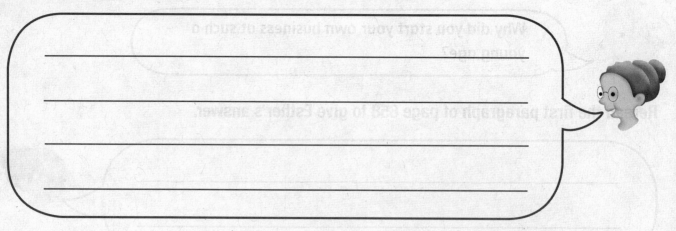

_____

_____

_____

_____

Adages and Proverbs

Underline the adage or proverb in each sentence. Then explain what it means in your own words.

1. Esther realized it's never too late to right a wrong.

   _____

2. When Esther wanted to get the right to vote, she knew that the longest journey starts with a single step.

   _____

3. In the Wyoming Territory, Esther found that a woman's work is never done.

   _____

4. Esther would not have listened to someone who said, "Don't rock the boat."

   _____

5. For Esther, there was no time like the present for getting the right to vote.

   _____

6. Esther seemed to believe that if at first you don't succeed, you should try again.

   _____

7. Esther proved that where there's a will, there's a way.

   _____

VCCV and VCV Patterns

Basic 1–11. Complete the puzzle by writing the Basic Word for each clue.

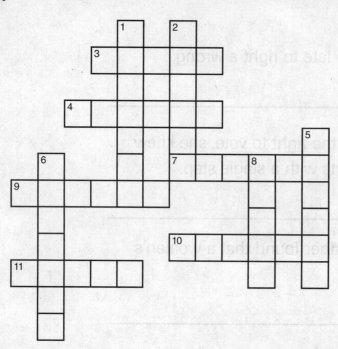

Spelling Words

1. dentist
2. final
3. finish
4. narrow
5. shelter
6. ahead
7. corner
8. hollow
9. divide
10. famous
11. recent
12. silver
13. capture
14. cabin
15. dinner
16. minus
17. minute
18. value
19. reward
20. broken

Challenge
decent
secure
standard
frontier
stampede

Across

3. in front of
4. having a space or opening inside
7. shiny, white metal
9. something given in return for a worthy act
10. sixty seconds
11. in math, to take away from

Down

1. something that protects or covers
2. very well known
5. not working properly
6. person qualified to treat people's teeth
8. to believe to be of worth

Challenge 12–14. You just watched a movie called "I Could Do That!" Describe a scene from the movie. Use three Challenge Words. Write on a separate sheet of paper.

Spelling Word Sort

Write each Basic Word beside the correct heading.

		Spelling Words
VC/CV Pattern: Divide Between the Consonants	**Basic Words:** **Challenge Words:** **Possible Selection Words:**	1. dentist 2. final 3. finish 4. narrow 5. shelter 6. ahead 7. corner 8. hollow 9. divide 10. famous
V/CV Pattern: Divide Before the Consonant	**Basic Words:** **Challenge Words:** **Possible Selection Words:**	11. recent 12. silver 13. capture 14. cabin 15. dinner 16. minus 17. minute
VC/V Pattern: Divide After the Consonant	**Basic Words:** **Possible Selection Words:**	18. value 19. reward 20. broken **Challenge** decent secure standard frontier stampede

Challenge Add the Challenge Words to your Word Sort.

Connect to Reading Look through "I Could Do That!" Find words that have the VCCV or VCV patterns on this page. Add them to your Word Sort.

Proofreading for Spelling

Find the misspelled words and circle them. Write them correctly on the lines below.

Susan B. Anthony was a famus woman at the end of the nineteenth century. In 1872, she broke the law by casting a vote in a presidential election. She knew that the resent Civil War had shown the valew of voting, a reaward that should be given to all people, not just men. She would devide her time between big cities and small towns. Susan wanted to captore the attention of women and convince them of their rights. Women would finich household chores early to host a tea or invite friends to diner just to discuss what Susan had to say. Susan would speak anywhere—a big meeting hall or a small kabin. Everywhere she went, there were crowds. Some women waited in line around the cornur for hours, while others stood along the nerrow hallways to catch Susan's finel words about civil and political rights.

1. _____   7. _____
2. _____   8. _____
3. _____   9. _____
4. _____   10. _____
5. _____   11. _____
6. _____   12. _____

Spelling Words

1. dentist
2. final
3. finish
4. narrow
5. shelter
6. ahead
7. corner
8. hollow
9. divide
10. famous
11. recent
12. silver
13. capture
14. cabin
15. dinner
16. minus
17. minute
18. value
19. reward
20. broken

Challenge

decent
secure
standard
frontier
stampede

Contractions with *not*

A **negative** is a word that makes a sentence mean *no*.
A negative contraction is made with a verb and the
negative word *not*. An apostrophe takes the place of
the letter *o* in each contraction with *not*.

contraction with *not*

Esther isn't at home, but she may be at the hat shop.

Thinking Question
What word is a contraction made with a verb and the negative word not?

1–8. Write the contraction for the underlined word or words in each sentence.

1. There <u>are not</u> any blue hats in the window today.
_____

2. This hat <u>does not</u> have a ribbon. _____

3. That small cowboy hat <u>will not</u> fit Mr. Fox's head.
_____

4. There <u>were not</u> many customers today. _____

5. The seamstress <u>cannot</u> find her sewing needle.
_____

6. Please <u>do not</u> sit on my hat. _____

7. Ms. Kelly <u>did not</u> buy the hat with red stripes.
_____

8. Esther <u>had not</u> made a hat this large before. _____

Using Negatives

The words *no*, *no one*, *nobody*, *none*, *nothing*, *nowhere*, and *never* are negatives. A contraction with a verb and the word *not* is also a negative. When making a negative statement, make sure to use just one negative.

positive

I understand the candidates' opinions.

negative

I <u>don't</u> understand the candidates' opinions.

I understand <u>none</u> of the candidates' opinions.

Thinking Questions
What word will change the sentence to have a negative meaning? Does the sentence still make sense?

1–6. Use a negative to change the meaning of the sentence from positive to negative. Write the negative sentence on the line below.

1. Anybody in the fifth grade can run for class president.

_____

2. Roger is running for class president.

_____

3. Tom has asked Roger if he can be his vice president.

_____

4. Myung-Yun always likes to help make campaign posters.

_____

5. Everyone is excited about the school elections this year.

_____

6. The class president can do something about all of the issues that bother students.

_____

_____

Avoiding Double Negatives

Words such as *not*, *no*, and *never* are negatives. Using two negatives together is called a **double negative**. Never use two negatives together in a sentence.

double negative

My mother won't tell nobody how she voted.

corrected sentences

My mother won't tell anybody how she voted.
My mother will tell nobody how she voted.

Thinking Question
What two negatives are used together in the sentence?

1–8. **Write the correct word shown in parentheses to complete the sentence.**

1. There (is, isn't) no presidential candidate that my parents completely support. _____

2. That candidate hasn't said (anything, nothing) about the important issues. _____

3. He doesn't support (any, none) of the laws to help the environment. _____

4. Don't vote for (anyone, no one) without learning his or her political views. _____

5. Doesn't (anybody, nobody) agree with that candidate's views? _____

6. Isn't there (anywhere, nowhere) I can get better information about the candidates? _____

7. The voters (have, haven't) no choice but to support the new law. _____

8. This candidate (has, hasn't) never been honest with the voters. _____

Relative Pronouns and Adverbs

The words *who*, *whose*, *whom*, *which*, and *that* can be used to begin clauses that explain *which one* or *what kind*. Other clauses explain *where*, *when*, and *why* about another clause.

Clause telling what kind of girl Esther was:
Esther was a smart girl **who wanted to do all she could.**

Clause telling why Esther wanted to do things:
When adults said, "Girls don't do that," Esther only wanted to do that thing more.

1–4. Underline the clause that tells which one or what kind.
Circle the word that begins the clause.

1. Esther was born into a family that included eleven children.

2. What made Esther different? She was a girl who was eager to learn.

3. As a young woman, Esther ran a millinery business that was very successful.

4. Votes for women was an idea whose time had come.

5–6. Underline the clause that tells where, when, or why. Circle the word that begins the clause.

5. In 1869, when she was fifty-five, Esther and two sons moved to Wyoming Territory.

6. The gold rush town where they settled had many men and few women.

Conventions

Name _____ Date _____

Proofreading can help you make certain that you have used contractions and negatives correctly in your writing.

---

incorrect, with proofreading marks

                                    was
Learning to sew ~~wasn't~~ never difficult for Esther.
                 ∧

correct

Learning to sew was never difficult for Esther.

1–6.   Correct the use of contractions or double negatives in each sentence.   Write the sentence correctly on the line below.

1. Esther doesnt' like that dress pattern.

_____

2. Esther never sewed nothing before she was eight.

_____

3. She couldn't find no silk for Ms. Kelly's dress.

_____

4. Sewing these pants wont take long.

_____

5. There isn't no one in town who sews better than Esther.

_____

6. The stitching on this shirt isnt neat and even.

_____

Focus Trait: Sentence Fluency
Using Transition Words

I Could Do That!
Writing: Informative Writing

Cause-and-Effect Sentences	Transition Added
When Esther was a girl, only men could vote. Her mother could not vote for president.	When Esther was a girl, only men could vote. **Therefore**, her mother could not vote for president.

Read each pair of sentences. Connect the ideas in the sentences using a cause-and-effect transition word or phrase.

Cause-and-Effect Sentences	Transition Added
1. Esther made nice clothes. Women paid her to make clothes for them.	Esther made nice clothes. _____ women paid her to make clothes for them.
2. Esther heard Susan B. Anthony speaking out about women's rights. She wanted to help women get the vote, too.	Esther heard Susan B. Anthony speaking out about women's rights, _____ she wanted to help women get the vote, too.

Pair/Share Work with a partner to brainstorm how to add transition words or phrases to make the sentences read smoothly.

Cause-and-Effect Sentences	Transition Added
3. Esther liked to do things for herself. She painted the sign for her hat shop.	
4. People thought that Esther was too young to run a business. They were shocked to see her open a hat shop.	

Name _____ Date _____

Lesson 23
READER'S NOTEBOOK

The Ever-Living Tree:
The Life and Times
of a Coast Redwood
Independent Reading

The Ever-Living Tree: The Life and Times of a Coast Redwood

Draw the Idea

Compare the events in the selection "The Ever-Living Tree: The Life and Times of a Coast Redwood."

Turn to page 687. Read the paragraph marked with the icon for Alexander the Great. What is the paragraph mainly about? How does the map help you understand the text?

_____

_____

Read the next paragraph on page 687 marked with the icon for the sequoia tree. What is the paragraph mainly about?
What do the layers of the tree show?

_____

_____

How are the main ideas of each section similar?

_____

_____

Why might the author have structured the text this way putting these ideas together?

_____

_____

Name _____ Date _____

Lesson 23
READER'S NOTEBOOK

The Ever-Living Tree:
The Life and Times
of a Coast Redwood

Independent Reading

Reread page 688. How are the ideas of the two sections similar?
Draw a picture of the Great Wall of China. Use at least one label to
show the idea shared between the sections.

Prefixes *pre-, inter-, ex-*

prearrange	interact	intermingle	ex-mayor
precaution	international	exceed	intercontinental

Each sentence shows a word in parentheses with the prefix *pre-*, *inter-*, or *ex-* in parentheses. Use each word in parentheses and your own words to complete each sentence.

1. (prearrange) I will call you to

_____

2. (precaution) Buckling your safety belt in the car is

_____

3. (interact) When you go to a new school,

_____

4. (international) The world-famous film actor was

_____

5. (intermingle) Because he's shy, he doesn't like it when

_____

6. (exceed) I know that your work will

_____

7. (ex-mayor) When the election comes,

_____

8. (intercontinental) The family traveled from North America
to South America

_____

Words with the VCCV Pattern

Basic 1–10. Write the Basic Word that each sentence describes.

1. No one else knows this.
   _____

2. Cats and dogs have these.
   _____

3. You buy this to see a movie in the theater.
   _____

4. Someone who writes a book is called this.
   _____

5. You can hang this on a wall for decoration.
   _____

6. You can put sand in this at the beach.
   _____

7. People travel into outer space using this.
   _____

8. This is a type of food to eat.
   _____

9. This protects your clothes when you cook.
   _____

10. This is to pick things up and put in one place.
   _____

Challenge 11–14. You have been invited to a friend's party, but you can't attend because you're going to your family reunion that day. Write a letter to your friend explaining why you can't attend the party. Use four Challenge Words. Write on a separate sheet of paper.

Spelling Words

1. poster
2. secret
3. whether
4. author
5. rocket
6. bushel
7. agree
8. bucket
9. ticket
10. declare
11. chicken
12. clothing
13. apron
14. whiskers
15. degree
16. gather
17. achieve
18. rather
19. bracket
20. machine

Challenge
regret
nephew
method
decline
vibrate

Spelling Word Sort

Write each Basic Word beside the correct heading.

		Spelling Words
V/CCV: Divide before the consonant blend or digraph	Basic Words: Challenge Words: Possible Selection Word:	1. poster 2. secret 3. whether 4. author 5. rocket 6. bushel 7. agree 8. bucket 9. ticket 10. declare
VCC/V: Divide after the consonant blend or digraph	Basic Words: Challenge Words: Possible Selection Words:	11. chicken 12. clothing 13. apron 14. whiskers 15. degree 16. gather 17. achieve 18. rather 19. bracket 20. machine

Challenge   Add the Challenge Words to your Word Sort.

Connect to Reading   Look through "The Ever-Living Tree: The Life and Times of a Coast Redwood." Find words that have the VCCV spelling pattern. Add them to your Word Sort.

Challenge
regret
nephew
method
decline
vibrate

Proofreading for Spelling

The Ever-Living Tree
Spelling: Words with the VCCV Pattern

Find the misspelled words and circle them. Write them correctly on the lines below.

In 1903, Colonel Charles Young was ordered to take his troops to Sequoia National Park. He would rathar have stayed in San Francisco, where the temperature rarely registered a degre under 45 in the winter. But whehter or not he wanted to go, he had to agre to the U.S. Army orders. Traveling on horseback for 16 days, Young and his troopers arrived in Sequoia. They brought clotheng and food. To make sure there was enough to eat, each man had to gathar a bushal of fruit and fill a buket with water. The supplies were so heavy the braket on the shelf broke. The men had no mashine to fix it. Hammer and nails would do. Young and his men were able to acheive their goal of making the wagon road long enough for people to be able to get to the park. Colonel Young, the first African-American superintendent of a national park, could deklare his work a success.

1. _____   7. _____

2. _____   8. _____

3. _____   9. _____

4. _____   10. _____

5. _____   11. _____

6. _____   12. _____

Spelling Words

1. poster
2. secret
3. whether
4. author
5. rocket
6. bushel
7. agree
8. bucket
9. ticket
10. declare
11. chicken
12. clothing
13. apron
14. whiskers
15. degree
16. gather
17. achieve
18. rather
19. bracket
20. machine

Challenge
regret
nephew
method
decline
vibrate

End of Sentence Punctuation

Different kinds of sentences end with different punctuation marks.

Kind of Sentence	End Punctuation	Example
statement or command	period (.)	Look at this tree. It is more than 500 years old.
question	question mark (?)	Have you ever planted a tree?
exclamation	exclamation mark (!)	What a remarkable life!

1–7.   **Write the appropriate end mark at the end of each sentence.**

1. Many animals live in and on trees _____

2. Do they harm the tree they call home _____

3. For the most part, they do not _____

4. However, some insect pests can kill a tree _____

5. What a spectacular leap that squirrel made _____

6. Look at the top branch of that tree _____

7. Is that a squirrel's nest I see _____

8–11.   **Rewrite the sentences on the lines. Use capital letters and end marks correctly.**

   our class is planting trees in the park today can you help us bring a shovel with you we are excited about this project

_____

_____

_____

Capital Letters and Punctuation in Quotations

Use capital letters and punctuation to write direct quotations correctly. Always capitalize the first word of a quotation. Use a comma to separate a quotation from the words that tell who is speaking. Put punctuation inside the last quotation marks.

When a quotation starts a sentence, put a comma at the end of a statement. Use the usual end punctuation for questions and exclamations.

direct quotations
Angela exlaimed, "What a big tree!"
"The redwood is a unique tree," Jee agreed.
"Do you think we can climb it?" asked Angela.

Thinking Questions
What kind of sentence is this quotation? Does the quotation come first or last in the sentence?

1–5.   Write the quotations correctly.

1. shall we look for something to eat the woodpecker asked

_____

2. the chipmunk asked do you see any acorns

_____

3. bugs sound good to me said the woodpecker.

_____

4. the chipmunk exclaimed that sounds absolutely awful

_____

5. most birds eat worms and bugs said the woodpecker

_____

Punctuation for Effect

Punctuation can show emotion or emphasize an idea.

Ellipses	To show tension, threat	It suddenly grew cold, and a raging wind ripped the branches. . . What would happen?
Exclamation mark (!)	To show surprise	A huge flash lit the forest!
Dash (—)	To emphasize	Lightning struck a pine tree—it was completely shattered in a flash.

1–4. Read each sentence. Rewrite it with appropriate punctuation on the lines. Capitalize the first word in each sentence.

1. we are going to a redwood forest an amazing place and we are really looking forward to it.

_____

_____

2. whoa look at the size of those creatures

_____

_____

3. they want to drive through the dark forest that sounds spooky to me

_____

_____

4. there's a bear coming run

_____

_____

Ordering Adjectives

Adjectives tell *which one*, *what kind*, or *how many* about a noun or pronoun.

What kind?	**Giant** trees may produce tiny seeds.
Which one?	**That** huge tree is a redwood.
How many?	**Numerous** redwoods were cut down.

When several adjectives describe one noun or pronoun, put them in order by category.

Number or Article	Opinion	Size, shape, age, color	Material	Purpose	Noun
The	beautiful	oval			brooch
One		ancient	gold		coin
Six	talented	young		basketball	players

1–3.   Complete each sentence with adjectives that answer the question in parentheses (   ).

1. (what kind?) The little tree spread its _____ roots far out.

2. (how many?) For _____ years, the tree remained small.

3. (which one?) _____ tree is the tallest tree in the forest.

4–5.   Choose three adjectives to describe each noun below. Be sure to put the adjectives in the correct order.

4. _____ bark

5. _____ needles

Conventions

> Use quotation marks around the exact words of a speaker. Place punctuation that ends the exact words inside the closing quotation marks. Words that name the speaker are set off by commas if they appear at the beginning or middle of the quotation. They end with a period if they come at the end of the sentence.
>
> "Have you seen my book?" asked Josh.
>
> "I saw it," said Dad, "in the the car."
>
> Josh recalled, "That's right. I took it to our campout last weekend."

Rewrite each sentence to add needed capital letters, quotation marks, and other missing punctuation. Use ellipses (…) and exclamation marks (!) for effect, where they are appropriate.

1. you have a lot of big trees in your yard said Jeff

   _____

2. Marla replied yes and we enjoy the shade they give us

   _____

3. did you know Marla asked that trees produce oxygen

   _____

4. wow look at that red-headed woodpecker exclaimed Jeff

   _____

Focus Trait: Organization
Writing Paragraphs

> A paragraph has sentences about one topic, such as how to do something. Writers organize their ideas or instructions to make them clear to the reader. For example, if you write directions, put the steps in the order they should be done. Use process transitions, such as *first* and *next*, to show the sequence of steps.

It is simple to make a tasty French toast breakfast. **First,** beat two eggs and half a cup of milk together until smooth. **Next,** dip each slice of bread into the egg mixture, turning it to coat both sides well. **Finally,** sprinkle cinnamon on the bread. Have an adult fry the slices in hot oil until they are brown.

Read the sentences below. Cross out any sentences that do not belong. Number the steps in order. Then write them in a paragraph on another sheet of paper. Put the directions in the correct order. Add transition words such as *first, next,* **and** *then.*

How to Plant a Tree

_____ Spread the seedling roots outward and downward while keeping the top of the root even with the top of the hole.

_____ Dig a hole large enough to hold the roots' full length.

_____ Give the planted seedling water and add mulch around its base.

_____ While holding the tree in place, fill the hole with dirt and tamp around the roots with your foot.

_____ Most bare-root seedlings are planted in the winter months.

Reader's Guide

Owen & Mzee

Trip to Haller Park

You are a scientist visiting Haller Park to find out more about hippos and tortoises. Take a close look at the following pages: 720 (to find out about where Owen lives), 722 (to find out what the animals eat and how they behave), 724 (for facts about tortoises and hippos).

Based on what you have read, write field notes about your observations. Remember that you are a scientist, so you want to focus on facts. What do you observe?

_____

_____

_____

_____

_____

_____

_____

_____

Name _____ Date _____

You focused on the facts—now how about your opinion? Your friends are not sure if they want to make the long trip to Haller Park to see Owen and Mzee. Should they visit? Why or why not? Write a postcard to a friend. Explain why Haller Park is—or is not—a great place to visit!

Suffixes -ed, -ly

wrapped	frequently	displayed	exhausted
normally	naturally	fairly	suffered

1–8 Complete each sentence using a word from the box.

1. It snows _____ in cold places like Alaska.

2. I would not _____ be so excited, but
   today is my birthday.

3. It is important to divide a treat _____ so
   that everyone gets the same amount.

4. After running ten miles, she was _____ .

5. During the spelling bee, he _____ the
   embarrassment of being on stage.

6. The books were _____ in the store
   window.

7. The actor read his lines very _____ .

8. _____ in a warm coat, I went out into the
   cold December snow.

Words with VCCCV Pattern

Owen and Mzee
Spelling: Words with VCCCV Pattern

Basic 1–12. Write the Basic Word that belongs in each group.

1. example, model, ____
2. stock, inventory, ____
3. describe, clarify, ____
4. locate, live, ____
5. traveler, seeker, ____
6. beast, creature, ____
7. empire, monarchy, ____
8. midpoint, halfway, ____
9. lone, solo, ____
10. sportsperson, player, ____
11. finish, conclude, ____
12. in place of, rather than, ____

Challenge 13–15. Write an e-mail message to your friend telling about an art exhibit you have seen—perhaps at an art museum, an art fair, or a school art exhibit. Use three Challenge Words. Write on a separate sheet of paper.

Spelling Words

1. hundred
2. supply
3. single
4. middle
5. explain
6. surprise
7. pilgrim
8. sandwich
9. instead
10. complete
11. monster
12. settle
13. address
14. farther
15. sample
16. although
17. turtle
18. athlete
19. orchard
20. kingdom

Challenge
fortress
instant
exclaim
mattress
sculptor

Spelling

316

Grade 4, Unit 5

© Houghton Mifflin Harcourt Publishing Company. All rights reserved.

Spelling Word Sort

Owen and Mzee
Spelling: Words with
VCCCV Pattern

Write each Basic Word beside the correct heading.

VC/CCV Pattern: Divide before consonant blend or digraph	Basic Words: Challenge Words: Possible Selection Words:
VCC/CV Pattern: Divide after consonant blend or digraph	Basic Words: Challenge Words: Possible Selection Words:

Spelling Words

1. hundred
2. supply
3. single
4. middle
5. explain
6. surprise
7. pilgrim
8. sandwich
9. instead
10. complete
11. monster
12. settle
13. address
14. farther
15. sample
16. although
17. turtle
18. athlete
19. orchard
20. kingdom

Challenge
fortress
instant
exclaim
mattress
sculptor

Challenge Add the Challenge Words to your Word Sort.

Connect to Reading Look through "Owen and Mzee: The True Story of a Remarkable Friendship." Find words that have the VCCCV patterns on this page. Add them to your Word Sort.

Owen and Mzee
Spelling: Words with
VCCCV Pattern

Proofreading for Spelling

Find the misspelled words and circle them. Write them correctly on the lines below.

This is a story about a rare hawksbill tirtle whose adress is Hanauma Bay Nature Preserve in Hawaii. The turtle was seen with a hook caught in its left flipper. Everyone assumed the turtle would die so it was a surprize when a scuba diver spotted it swimming farthur out in the bay. Divers were able to rescue the hawksbill, altheugh the vet's X-ray showed a sengle rusty fishing hook embedded in the animal. The vet decided to cut away as much of the hook as possible insteed of removing it. After the hawksbill was treated with antibiotics, it was released back into Hanauma Bay with "HB" painted on its shell. Several hundrid people visit the bay daily. Some will bring a sandwitch and fruit from a nearby orcherd. They hope to catch a glimpse of "HB" swimming in the midle of the bay.

1. _____   7. _____
2. _____   8. _____
3. _____   9. _____
4. _____   10. _____
5. _____   11. _____
6. _____

Spelling Words

1. hundred
2. supply
3. single
4. middle
5. explain
6. surprise
7. pilgrim
8. sandwich
9. instead
10. complete
11. monster
12. settle
13. address
14. farther
15. sample
16. although
17. turtle
18. athlete
19. orchard
20. kingdom

Challenge

fortress
instant
exclaim
mattress
sculptor

Commas with Direct Speech and Names

When you write, use a comma to set off the name of a person addressed directly and to set off introductory words such as *yes*, *no*, and *well*.

Yolanda, can you tell me about the giant tortoise?
Well, the giant tortoise eats both plants and animals.
I wonder, Mr. Scorzo, if a tortoise is the same as a turtle?

Thinking Questions
Does the sentence include an introductory word or the name of a person being addressed? Does the quotation include words that tell who is speaking?

1–5. Write the sentences correctly. Add commas where they are needed.

1. Yes giant tortoises sleep inside their shells.

_____

_____

2. Randy have you ever picked up a tortoise?

_____

_____

3. No I would be afraid it might bite me.

_____

_____

4. These animals cannot walk fast Brenda though their legs are strong.

_____

_____

5. Well their legs have to hold up those very heavy shells.

_____

_____

Commas in Compound Sentences

A **compound sentence** joins two complete ideas using a coordinating conjunction such as *and*, *but*, *or*, or *so*. Each half of a compound sentence has its own subject and predicate. Use a comma before the conjunction in a compound sentence.

Thinking Questions
Which word is the coordinating conjunction? Where does the comma go in the sentence?

       subject   verb   subject verb
Hippopotamuses <u>live</u> in lakes and rivers, **but** they <u>graze</u> on land every day.

1–3. **Join each pair of sentences using the conjunction in parentheses ( ). Be sure your compound sentence has a comma before the conjunction.**

1. Hippos graze for hours each evening. They eat up to 150 pounds of food a day. (and)

_____

_____

2. Hippos have eyes, ears, and nose on the top of their heads. They can keep most of their body underwater. (so)

_____

_____

3. Hippos cannot sweat. They keep cool in the mud and water. (but)

_____

_____

_____

More Uses of Commas

Use a comma to separate the words in a series.

We saw <u>tortoises</u>, <u>hippopotamuses</u>, and <u>birds</u>.
There are <u>sea lions</u>, <u>sea otters</u>, <u>fur seals</u>, and <u>elephant seals</u> at the zoo.
Use a comma between a date and a year.
Today is <u>May 4, 2013</u>.
Use a comma between a city and a state.
I live in <u>Glendale, Arizona</u>.

Thinking Questions
How are commas used to separate items in a series? How are commas used in dates and place names?

1–4. **Add commas where they are needed. Write the sentence correctly on the line.**

1. My report on the marine sanctuary is due on December 12 2014.

_____

_____

2. People who drill dump or dig up the sea floor are not allowed in the sanctuary.

_____

_____

3. The sanctuary is located in Monterey California.

_____

4. A layer of fat a thick coat of fur and a dry spot in the sun all help sea mammals to stay warm.

_____

_____

Relative Pronouns and Adverbs

A **dependent clause** has a subject and verb, but it cannot stand alone. A dependent clause is joined to an **independent clause** that expresses a complete thought. The relative pronouns *who, whom, whose, that,* and *which* begin dependent clauses that answer the question *Which one?* or *What kind?* Relative adverbs begin dependent clauses that tell *where, when* or *why.*

Dependent clause beginning with relative pronoun

A hippopotamus is a fierce fighter **that** protects its young.

Dependent clause beginning with relative adverb

The mother springs into action **when** her baby is attacked.

1–8. Underline the dependent clause in each sentence. Circle the relative adverb or relative pronoun that begins the clause.

1. Many hippos lost their lives when a tsunami struck the African coast.

2. The only hippo who survived was a six-hundred-pound baby named Owen.

3. Owen badly needed a mother whom he could trust and learn from.

4. Rescuers were not sure where Owen should go.

5. Haller Park was the animal sanctuary where Owen was given a home.

6. The giant tortoise Mzee at first thought that Owen should leave him alone.

7. The two soon became friends who could not be separated.

8. No one knows for sure why Owen and Mzee became such good friends.

Sentence Fluency

Proofreading can help you make certain that you have used commas correctly in your writing. Using commas makes your writing clear and easy to understand.

Incorrect with proofreading marks

Mark: You know, Dad the population of hippos in Africa has shrunk tremendously.

Dad: That's a serious problem Mark.

Correct

Mark: You know, Dad, the population of hippos in Africa has shrunk tremendously.

Dad: That's a serious problem, Mark.

Activity   This part of a script has 16 missing commas. Add a comma or commas to each part in the script.

Mark: Yes I agree. Did you know Dad that people are the greatest
        threat to the hippo population?

Dad: No I wasn't aware of that.

Mark: Well it's true. Hippos are killed for their fat their ivory teeth and because
        they eat so much grass.

Dad: Is anything being done to save the hippos Mark?

Mark: Yes some of the areas where hippos live are protected.

Dad: Well that makes sense. I think Mark that we should do our
        part to save the hippos.

Mark: That's a great idea Dad! Let's get a hippo for a pet!

Dad: No let's not. You were kidding weren't you Mark?

Owen and Mzee
Writing: Informative Writing

Focus Trait: Ideas
Finding the Best Information

Source	Information
Encyclopedia	Articles about many different topics
Atlas	Maps of places all over the world
Internet	Web sites of organizations as well as electronic reference materials
Interviewing an expert	Unique information
Newspaper and magazine articles	Up-to-date information on different topics
Nonfiction books	Facts about real people, places, and things

1–3. Answer the following questions about using sources to find the best information.

1. Maggie is researching tortoises. She wants to answer the question, *Where do tortoises live?*

   a. Which source could Maggie use? _____

   b. What other question could she answer by using this source?

   _____

2. Luis is researching how zoos are run. He wants to answer the question, *How many people work at the zoo in my city?*

   a. Which source should Luis use? _____

   b. What other question could he answer with this source?

   _____

3. Nina is researching Kenya. She wants to answer the question, *What ocean is closest to Kenya?*

   a. Which source should Nina use? _____

   b. What other question could she answer with this source?

   _____

The Fun They Had: from *Isaac Asimov: The Complete Stories*

I Want a Live Teacher!

Margie would like to try learning the old-fashioned way, from a live teacher. She is writing an e-mail to the Inspector to try and convince him to give up the mechanical teacher. But Margie understands that she should use language with which the Inspector is comfortable.

Look closely at the way the Inspector talks on page 749. Help Margie finish her e-mail using the formal language that the Inspector uses.

New Message
To: Inspector
From: Margie
Subject: Replacing the Mechanical Teacher

Dear Inspector:

I am writing to you to suggest that you remove the mechanical teacher from my home and let me learn from a human teacher instead.

_____

_____

_____

_____

Sincerely,

Margie

Name _____ Date _____

Lesson 25
READER'S NOTEBOOK

The Fun They Had: from
Isaac Asimov:
The Complete Stories
Independent Reading

Margie would like Tommy to take classes with her from a
human teacher. She e-mails him to ask for his help in changing
to a human teacher.

Look closely at the way Margie and Tommy talk to each other on
page 750. Help Margie finish her e-mail using the informal language
that they use.

New Message

To: **Tommy**

From: **Margie**

Subject: **Replacing the Mechanical Teacher**

Hey Tommy!

I have an idea that you can help me with. We could get rid of the stupid
mechanical teacher and get a real person to teach us!

_____

_____

_____

_____

_____

_____

_____

Your buddy,

Margie

Greek and Latin Word Parts
meter, therm, aud, fac

The words in the box each have a part that comes from Greek or Latin. In Greek, *therm* means "heat" and *meter* means "measure." In Latin, *aud* means "to hear" and *fac* means "to make" or "to do."

thermometer	barometer	audible	manufacture
thermal	chronometer	audience	factory

1–8 Write the correct word from the box to complete each sentence.

1. When the concert ended, the orchestra stood and bowed to the _____.

2. The captain used a _____ to help determine the ship's time of departure.

3. The automobile plant will _____ cars.

4. Check the _____ outside to see if you need a sweater.

5. Mr. Wilson makes chocolate candy at his _____.

6. The weather forecast predicts rain, because the _____ reading shows a drop in air pressure.

7. The park ranger wears his _____ socks in winter to keep warm.

8. With everyone talking at once, Solomon's voice was barely _____ above the noise.

Words with VV Pattern

The Fun They Had
Spelling: Words with VV Pattern

Basic 1–10. Write the Basic Words that fit the clues to complete the crossword puzzle.

Spelling Words

1. idea
2. lion
3. usual
4. radio
5. liar
6. poem
7. India
8. piano
9. January
10. quiet
11. poet
12. science
13. diary
14. violin
15. period
16. February
17. cereal
18. video
19. meteor
20. rodeo

Challenge

variety
gradual
geography
diagram
punctuate

Across

6. piece of rock flying through space
8. tape that records TV programs
9. where cowhands show skills
10. equipment used to receive signals

Down

1. study of natural things
2. food made from grain
3. second month of the year
4. punctuation mark
5. large musical instrument
7. daily written record

Challenge 11–14. You are asked to be student teacher for your geography class today. Give instructions to the class about a writing assignment in which they describe the features of the region in which they live. Use four of the Challenge Words. Write on a separate sheet of paper.

Spelling Word Sort

The Fun They Had
Spelling: Words with VV Pattern

Write each Basic Word beside the correct heading.

VV Pattern with two syllables: Divide between the vowels	**Basic Words:**
	Possible Selection Words:
VV Pattern with three syllables: Divide between the vowels	**Basic Words:**
	Challenge Words:
VV Pattern with four syllables: Divide between the vowels	**Basic Words:**
	Challenge Words:
	Possible Selection Words:

Challenge   Add the Challenge Words to your Word Sort.

Connect to Reading   Look through "The Fun They Had." Find words that have the VV patterns on this page. Add them to your Word Sort.

Spelling Words

1. idea
2. lion
3. usual
4. radio
5. liar
6. poem
7. India
8. piano
9. January
10. quiet
11. poet
12. science
13. diary
14. violin
15. period
16. February
17. cereal
18. video
19. meteor
20. rodeo

Challenge
variety
gradual
geography
diagram
punctuate

Name _____ Date _____

Proofreading for Spelling

Find the misspelled words and circle them. Write them correctly on the lines below.

It was in Janeary that Talia got the idear to enter the Galactic Music Contest. She wrote a composition for her violen using a pome for inspiration. It was early Febuary when she heard.

"Mamma, guess what?" said Talia, smiling. "I placed in the contest. I have to go to Indea for the final competition. I may get to see a lyin there!"

"That's wonderful news," said Mrs. Simms as she handed Talia the sereal.

Talia left the next morning on the shuttle. Everyone was quiat and focused on the captain's vidio. She explained that in the usueal way, after blast-off, they would shut off the engines to conserve fuel and switch to solar power. As Talia looked out the window, she saw a metear streak past her. To her, that was a sign of good luck!

1. _____	7. _____
2. _____	8. _____
3. _____	9. _____
4. _____	10. _____
5. _____	11. _____
6. _____	12. _____

Spelling Words

1. idea
2. lion
3. usual
4. radio
5. liar
6. poem
7. India
8. piano
9. January
10. quiet
11. poet
12. science
13. diary
14. violin
15. period
16. February
17. cereal
18. video
19. meteor
20. rodeo

Challenge
variety
gradual
geography
diagram
punctuate

Capitalization and Writing Titles

Capitalize important words in the titles of movies, books, chapters, and articles in a newspaper or magazine. Short words such as *in*, *if*, *of*, *a*, and *the* are not capitalized unless they are the first word in the title.

When writing the title of a shorter work, such as a story or news article, use quotation marks. When writing the title of a longer work, such as a book, magazine, or movie, underline the title.

book title   **story**
<u>A Pizza for Jin</u>   "The Diary of a Mouse"

Thinking Questions
Which words in this title should be capitalized? Does the title name a long work or a short work?

1–4. Rewrite each sentence. Add capital letters, underlining, and punctuation where they are needed.

1. The headline in Friday's newspaper read "clowns lead parade."

_____

_____

2. the little mermaid is my little sister's favorite movie.

_____

_____

3. Jesse's story about his trip to Mexico was called "crossing the border."

_____

_____

4. benson elementary wins trophy was the front page headline in the school paper.

_____

_____

End Punctuation

The punctuation at the end of a sentence helps to show its meaning. Use a period (.) at the end of a statement or a command. Use a question mark (?) at the end of a question and an exclamation mark (!) to show strong feeling.

Thinking Questions
What kind of sentence is it? Does the sentence tell something, ask a question, or show excitement?

declarative	I like to play basketball.
imperative	Hand me the ball, please.
interrogative	What is the score?
exclamatory	What a great game!

1–8. Add the correct end mark for each sentence. Write *declarative*, *interrogative*, *imperative*, or *exclamatory* on the line.

1. A voice command can make the mechanical dog walk and sit _____

2. Insert a quarter into the machine _____

3. How many centuries have passed since the Revolutionary War _____

4. The building inspector will come here to check next week _____

5. Your picture is amazing _____

6. What a waste of time this is _____

7. How much progress have you made with your work _____

8. Try not to miss your bus _____

Commas Before Coordinating Conjunctions

A compound sentence joins two independent clauses using the coordinating conjunctions *and*, *but*, *or*, *nor*, *for*, or *so*. Use a comma before the conjunction.

The <u>children</u> were curious about the book, **for** <u>they</u> <u>had</u> never <u>seen</u> one.
<u>Children</u> <u>can learn</u> in a classroom, **or** <u>they</u> <u>can learn</u> through computer lessons.

Thinking Questions
How many independent clauses are in the sentence? What word should connect the clauses?

1–4. **Join each pair of sentences to make a compound sentence using the conjunction shown in parentheses. Use commas correctly.**

1. Computers are here to stay. They run many systems in our society. (and)

   _____

   _____

2. Schools might become unnecessary. Each child may be taught by a machine. (for)

   _____

   _____

3. Any book could be put on a computer. Books might also disappear. (so)

   _____

4. Computer school would be convenient. I would miss books and teachers. (but)

   _____

   _____

Name _____ Date _____

Use Quotation Marks and Other Punctuation Marks

When writing someone's exact words, enclose them in quotation marks (""). Capitalize the first word of a quotation. Use a comma to separate a quotation from the words that tell who is speaking. Put end marks inside the last quotation marks. When a quotation starts a sentence, put a comma at the end of a statement instead of a period. If the quotation ends with a question mark or exclamation point, a comma is not used.

Tommy cried, "Look! I found a real book!"
"Where on Earth did you find that?" asked Margie.
"I searched for days," Tommy replied.

1–5. Rewrite each quotation. Add the punctuation marks and capital letters that are needed.

1. My computerized teacher is broken said Margie

_____

2. Why don't we read this book instead suggested Tommy.

_____

3. But it's so heavy exclaimed Margie.

_____

4. Tommy said I like turning the paper pages.

_____

5. Margie added they feel cool and crisp.

_____

Conventions

Incorrect Mechanics	Correct Mechanics
At last! the day of the science fair has finally arrived and everyones excited. mr. joness class will present it's project first? Our class will be last.	At last! The day of the science fair has finally arrived, and everyone's excited. Mr. Jones's class will present its project first. Our class will be last.

1–4. **Rewrite the sentences on the lines below. Use the correct capitalization and punctuation.**

1. dont forget to bring treats to school on Friday. they are for Miss Smiths birthday party

   _____

   _____

2. simons boots were covered with mud they were also filthy and smelly

   _____

   _____

3. be careful didnt I tell you the sidewalk was slippery its covered with ice, too

   _____

   _____

4. kim wrote a scary story about an imaginary friend named Bindi its called the secret staircase

   _____

   _____

Focus Trait: Word Choice
Using Precise Language

Sentence Using General Language	Sentence Using Precise Language
The computer screen said things, and Margie put her work into a slot.	The computer's monitor flashed commands, and Margie slid her homework on a disk into a gleaming slot.

1–4. The sentences below are vague and overly general. Rewrite each sentence to use precise language about computers.
Use some words from the box to help you be more precise.
If necessary, look up these words in a dictionary.

browser	microchip	data	memory	hard drive	Internet
memory	monitor	software	CPU	keyboard	browse

1. A computer stores information and lets users find more information.

_____

_____

2. A computer's brain is on these little pieces that carry electricity and hold information.

_____

_____

3. A computer contains programs that tell it what to do.

_____

_____

4. Information appears on a screen.

_____

_____

The Girl Who Loved Spiders

Dear Dr. Help

Imagine that Luis is so afraid of spiders he writes to an advice columnist for help just after he moves to Florida. Take a close look at pages 4 and 5. What would Luis say about why he is afraid of spiders?

Dear Dr. Help,

_____

_____

_____

_____

_____

_____

How can I get over my fear of spiders?
Thanks,
Luis

Name _____ Date _____

Lesson 26
READER'S NOTEBOOK

The Girl Who Loved
Spiders
Independent Reading

Now take a close look at pages 7, 9, and 11. Imagine that you are the advice columnist responding to Luis. Using what you learned from the selection, what would you tell Luis?

Dear Luis,

_____

_____

_____

_____

_____

_____

_____

Good luck!

Dr. Help

Final Schwa + /r/ Sounds

Basic 1–16.   Write the Basic Word that best fits each clue.

1. One of five digits on each hand: __ __ ◯ __ __ __
2. A person who acts in a play: __ __ __ ◯ __
3. A kind act that helps a friend: __ __ ◯ __ __
4. Disturb: __ __ __ __ ◯ __
5. Provides power to a car: ◯ __ __ __ __
6. A sign with words or a design: ◯ __ __ __ __ __
7. A body temperature higher than normal: __ ◯ __ __ __
8. Shows your reflection: __ __ __ ◯ __ __
9. Treats people who are sick: ◯ __ __ __ __ __
10. Come into: ◯ __ __ __ __
11. Part of a shirt that fits around your neck: ◯ __ __ __ __ __
12. Sprays water to clean: __ __ __ __ ◯ __
13. A person's state of mind: __ __ __ ◯ ◯ __ __
14. Person who begs for a living: ◯ __ __ __ __ __
15. Can be worn for warmth: __ __ ◯ __ __ __
16. Hard work: __ __ __ ◯ __

Now write the circled letters in order to name two months of the year.

Answer: __ __ __ __ __ __ __ __ and

__ __ __ __ __ __ __ __

Challenge 17–18.   Write a sentence using two of the Challenge Words. Write on a separate sheet of paper.

Spelling Words

Basic
1. enter
2. banner
3. sugar
4. shower
5. motor
6. collar
7. labor
8. finger
9. mirror
10. beggar
11. favor
12. bother
13. fever
14. doctor
15. temper
16. actor
17. polar
18. sweater
19. traitor
20. whenever

Challenge
calendar
error
popular
barrier
director

Word Sort

Write each Basic Word next to the correct heading.

final /ər/ spelled *ar*	Basic Words: Challenge Words:
final /ər/ spelled *er*	Basic Words: Challenge Word: Possible Selection Words:
final /ər/ spelled *or*	Basic Words: Challenge Words: Possible Selection Word:

Challenge   Add the Challenge Words to your Word Sort.

Connect to Reading   Look through "The Girl Who Loved Spiders." Find words that have the final schwa + /r/ spelling patterns. Add them to your Word Sort.

Spelling Words

Basic
1. enter
2. banner
3. sugar
4. shower
5. motor
6. collar
7. labor
8. finger
9. mirror
10. beggar
11. favor
12. bother
13. fever
14. doctor
15. temper
16. actor
17. polar
18. sweater
19. traitor
20. whenever

Challenge
calendar
error
popular
barrier
director

Name _____ Date _____

Proofreading for Spelling

Find the misspelled words and circle them. Write them correctly on the lines below.

I pulled the coller of my sweeter up around my ears. Even though I had a fevre, I still felt cold. I needed a docter. Instead a polor bear walked up to me and said, "Whennever I look in the miror, I see shugar. Is that normal?" The bear was wearing a red shirt and blue jeans. I reached out my hand to touch him. He felt real. Maybe I was sicker than I thought.

I told him he shouldn't bothar me with silly questions. Then I asked if he was real or an actur. He lost his tempir and called me a trator to the cause. He held up a bannor that said "Bears Should Rule the World," wagged his fingir at me, and left. Then the door opened and my mom came in to check on me. She sighed and said, "You are burning up!" I took my sweater off and went to sleep.

1. _____   8. _____

2. _____   9. _____

3. _____   10. _____

4. _____   11. _____

5. _____   12. _____

6. _____   13. _____

7. _____   14. _____

Spelling Words

Basic
1. enter
2. banner
3. sugar
4. shower
5. motor
6. collar
7. labor
8. finger
9. mirror
10. beggar
11. favor
12. bother
13. fever
14. doctor
15. temper
16. actor
17. polar
18. sweater
19. traitor
20. whenever

Challenge
calendar
error
popular
barrier
director

Making Comparisons

<u>Comparative adjectives</u> are used to compare two things.
<u>Superlative adjectives</u> are used to compare more than two things.

Adjective	Comparative	Superlative
slow	slower	slowest
cute	cuter	cutest
fast	faster	fastest
happy	happier	happiest

Thinking Question
How many persons, places, or things are being compared?

A turtle is *slower* than a lizard.

A snail is the *slowest* of the three.

1–6. Circle the correct form of the adjective to complete each sentence. Write C if the adjective is the comparative form. Write S if the adjective is the superlative form.

1. Jana is (tall, taller) than her sister Sasha. _____

2. My little sister is the (cutest, cuter) baby in the whole world.

   _____

3. Kelli insisted that ghost stories are (scariest, scarier) to read

   than biographies. _____

4. That is the (funnier, funniest) joke I have ever heard. _____

5–6. Matt is a (fastest, faster) runner than Saleem, but Juan is the

   (fastest, faster) runner of the three boys. _____

Making Comparisons with *more* and *most*

With long adjectives, use *more* to compare two persons, places, or things. Use *most* to compare three or more.

The ant is **more** interesting than the grasshopper.
The ant is the **most** interesting of all insects.

Thinking Question
How many persons, places, or things are being compared?

1–5. Rewrite each sentence, adding either *more* or *most* to the adjective in parentheses.

1. The _____ things I learned to do when I moved to Florida were to always wear shoes, to always shake out my shoes, and to watch my step when walking. (important)

_____

_____

_____

2. Spiders are _____ in Florida than in New York. (plentiful)

_____

_____

3. I think the _____ part about moving is making new friends. (difficult)

_____

_____

4. I think running road races is _____ than looking for bugs. (satisfying)

_____

_____

5. What is the _____ insect to be found in the area where you live? (common)

_____

_____

Name _____ Date _____

Lesson 26
READER'S NOTEBOOK

The Girl Who
Loved Spiders

Grammar: Making Comparisons

Comparing with *good* and *bad*

Some adjectives need to change forms when they are used to compare things.

The adjectives *good* and *bad* are two examples.

Adjective	Comparative	Superlative
good	better	best
bad	worse	worst

Thinking Question
How many persons, places, or things are being compared?

Getting out of school early is good. Weekends are better. Summer break is best of all.

1–5. Complete the sentence by writing the correct form of the adjective shown in parentheses.

1. The _____ news I heard was that 120 amphibian
   species are now extinct. (bad)

2. David was happy that his second paper was _____ than
   his first. (good)

3. What is the _____ book you have ever read? (good)

4. I liked the first book _____ than the second. (good)

5. The _____ part of our museum trip was the ride home.
   (bad)

Name _____ Date _____

Lesson 26
READER'S NOTEBOOK

The Girl Who
Loved Spiders
Grammar: Spiral Review

Correct Adjectives

- The words *a, an,* and *the* are special adjectives called **articles.**

Articles	
Use *a* if the next word begins with a consonant sound.	Ron found **a** giant beetle.
Use *an* if the next word begins with a vowel sound.	**An** ant is a social insect.
Use *the* if the noun names a particular person, place, or thing.	**The** grasshopper landed right on Maria's book.

- Capitalize adjectives formed from proper nouns.

    Wayne studied **Amazon** ants.

1–5.   Rewrite the sentences, supplying the correct article.

1. Roberto wrote ____ report on dragonflies.

_____

2. _____ class visited a museum last Thursday.

_____

3–4. The spider is ____ arachnid and not ___ insect.

_____

5. I want to learn everything I can about _____ moth.

_____

6–8.   Rewrite the sentences, correcting errors in the use of proper adjectives.

6. The canadian guide told us what to look for.

_____

7. The arabian horse has great energy and intelligence.

_____

8. For a solid week the group investigated the mexican coast.

_____

_____

Sentence Fluency

Combine two short, choppy sentences into one
sentence to make sentences flow smoothly.

Sentence 1	Sentence 2
The elephant is the biggest animal in the zoo.	The elephant is also the most magnificent animal.

The elephant is the biggest and most magnificent animal in the zoo.

1–3. Combine these short, choppy sentences to make one sentence.

1.

Sentence 1	Sentence 2
The Taipan snake has the most poisonous venom of any snake in Australia.	It also has the longest fangs.

_____

_____

2.

Sentence 1	Sentence 2
The largest shark on the Australian coast is the great white.	It is also the scariest shark.

_____

_____

3.

Sentence 1	Sentence 2
My science teacher, Mrs. Welles, is the most interesting teacher I have ever had.	She also is the most knowledgable.

_____

_____

Focus Trait: Word Choice
Precise Language

As you describe the characters, setting, and plot in your response, choose clear, exact words to show the reader clearly the features of the story.

Topic	Exact Details
Characters	fascinating, realistic, sympathetic, evil

List three or more details that you might use to express your opinion about the following parts of a story you have read recently. Include interesting word choice.

Topic	Exact Details
1. Place	
2. Time	
3. Events	
4. Ending	

Reader's Guide

Amphibian Alert!

Amphibian Conservation Group

Suppose you work for a conservation group working to protect amphibians. Help create a pamphlet about your organization.

On this side of the pamphlet, tell why your group exists. Look closely at pages 22–23 (to find details that tell what amphibians are and where they live) and pages 24 and 25 (to find details about threats to amphibian life). Use two synonyms for the noun *threat* in your pamphlet.

What Is an Amphibian?

_____

_____

_____

Threats to Amphibian Life:

_____

_____

_____

_____

_____

_____

Name _____ Date _____

On this side of the pamphlet, tell what people can do to help
protect amphibians. Look closely at pages 26 and 27 to find details
to help you write. Use two antonyms for the word *threaten* in this
part of the pamphlet. Remember, you work for a conservation group.

What Conservation Groups Do:

_____

_____

_____

_____

What You Can Do to Help:

_____

_____

_____

_____

_____

_____

The Final Schwa + /l/ Sound

Basic 1–10. Read the paragraphs. Write the Basic Words that would best replace the numbers in parentheses to complete the sentences.

Spelling Words

Basic

1. title
2. towel
3. battle
4. pedal
5. metal
6. simple
7. eagle
8. special
9. total
10. trouble
11. nickel
12. gentle
13. barrel
14. model
15. tangle
16. ankle
17. marvel
18. juggle
19. squirrel
20. riddle

It was an exciting and (**1**) day. Ana arrived at a bicycle race. She stopped to (**2**) at the colorful balloons and streamers decorating the starting line. A (**3**) of ten other racers were standing by their bicycles.

"Don't be nervous," Ana told herself. "This will be (**4**) compared to all the training that I did."

Ana remembered to tie her shoelaces so they would not (**5**) in her bicycle wheels. The last time that had happened, Ana hurt her (**6**). Ana used a (**7**) to wipe mud off the shiny (**8**) bicycle frame.

At the starting line, Ana prepared to (**9**) fast. She and the other racers burst forward. It was going to be a (**10**) for the prize!

1. _____   6. _____
2. _____   7. _____
3. _____   8. _____
4. _____   9. _____
5. _____   10. _____

Challenge

cancel
decimal
material
pretzel
triangle

Challenge 11–12. Imagine that your teacher asks you to write about your favorite subject, which is math. Use two of the Challenge Words. Write on a separate sheet of paper.

Word Sort

Write each Basic Word next to the correct heading.

Final /l/ or /əl/ sound spelled *el*	Basic Words: Challenge Words:
Final /l/ or /əl/ sound spelled *al*	Basic Words: Challenge Words: Possible Selection Word:
Final /l/ or /əl/ sound spelled *le*	Basic Words: Challenge Word: Possible Selection Words:

Challenge: Add the Challenge Words to your Word Sort.

Connect to Reading: Look through "Amphibian Alert!" Find words that have the final schwa + /l/ spelling patterns on this page. Add them to your Word Sort.

Spelling Words

Basic
1. title
2. towel
3. battle
4. pedal
5. metal
6. simple
7. eagle
8. special
9. total
10. trouble
11. nickel
12. gentle
13. barrel
14. model
15. tangle
16. ankle
17. marvel
18. juggle
19. squirrel
20. riddle

Challenge
cancel
decimal
material
pretzel
triangle

Proofreading for Spelling

Find the misspelled words and circle them. Write them correctly on the lines below.

In 1799, a French army officer named Pierre-Francois Bouchard was working near the city of Rosetta in Egypt. Bouchard and his men saw many ancient things, including a moddel of a house made of a mettal that looked like nikel. For fun, the men would juggil small stones. One day Bouchard found a stone slab that was different from the others. He was very gentil with it as he used water from a nearby barel to wash off the layers of dirt.

Bouchard saw strange symbols. The treuble was that he did not know what they meant. Bouchard took the stone to scholars. They all had to marvell at it, but they were unable to understand it. Was that a reddle or the titil of a play? Was the bird an eagel? Was that little creature a flying squerrel? More than 20 years passed before anyone could translate the Rosetta Stone.

Spelling Words

1. title
2. towel
3. battle
4. pedal
5. metal
6. simple
7. eagle
8. special
9. total
10. trouble
11. nickel
12. gentle
13. barrel
14. model
15. tangle
16. ankle
17. marvel
18. juggle
19. squirrel
20. riddle

Challenge
cancel
decimal
material
pretzel
triangle

1. _____ 7. _____

2. _____ 8. _____

3. _____ 9. _____

4. _____ 10. _____

5. _____ 11. _____

6. _____ 12. _____

Comparing with *good* and *bad*

Comparative *Good* and *Bad*: Use *better* or *worse* to compare two things.
Superlative: Use *best* or *worst* to compare three or more things.

Thinking Questions
Is the comparison comparative *or* superlative? *What form of* good *or* bad *should be used to compare?*

Adjective	Comparative	Superlative
good	better	best
bad	worse	worst

Brad earned a **better** score than Jake, but Amelia earned the **best** grade of all.

Circle the correct form of the word in parentheses. Write C if the word is the comparative form. Write S for the superlative form.

1. John's ideas were (best, better) than Dave's to improve the amphibian display. _____

2. Sean had the (worse, worst) job—repairing the frog terrariums. _____

3. Team A's display was (worst, worse) than team B's. _____

4. Of all the guides at the amphibian display, Marta explains tadpoles (better, best). _____

Comparing with Adverbs

For most adverbs that end in *-ly*:
- use *more* to compare two actions.
- use *most* to compare three or more actions.

Thinking Question
Does the adverb end in -ly? How many things does the adverb compare?

Adverb	Comparative	Superlative
quickly	more quickly	most quickly
skillfully	more skillfully	most skillfully
easily	more easily	most easily

A horse runs **more quickly** than a human. Cheetahs run the **most quickly** of all animals.

1–5. **Write the form of the adverb shown in parentheses that correctly completes the sentence.**

1. Do you think turtles can swim _____ than frogs? (quickly)

2. The third doctor cared for the injured newt _____. (skillfully)

3. Jason handles the salamanders _____ than Bill. (carefully)

4. Of all the helpers, Aiden works the _____. (quietly)

5. Alan identified amphibians _____ than Mitsuo after taking a class. (easily)

Making Comparisons

1–6. **Circle the correct word in parentheses to complete each sentence.**

1. Dennis smiles (wider, widest) of all his friends.

2. "I think clothing dries (most, more) quickly in warm air than
   in cold," said Dana.

3. I shop at Bloom's Market (more, most) frequently than
   I shop at Lynn's Market.

4. Of all the fruits sold at Bloom's market, the bananas will
   (more, most) likely sell out first.

5–6. When teams choose players, Beth is (most, more) readily
   chosen than Brianne because she runs (faster, fastest).

Negatives

- A word that makes a sentence mean "no" is called a *negative*.
- The words *no, no one, nobody, none, nothing,* and *never* are negatives.
- The word *not* and contractions made from *not* are also negatives.
- Never use two negatives together in a sentence.

Incorrect	Correct
There **weren't no** fish in the pond.	There **weren't any** fish in the pond. There **were no** fish in the pond.
I **won't never** give away my frog.	I **won't ever** give away my frog. I **will never** give away my frog.

1–4. Write the negative on the line provided.

1. Nobody wanted to leave. _____

2. I can't finish this assignment on time. _____

3. Before this class, I had never studied reptiles. _____

4. I had no interest in learning about newts. _____

5–8. Rewrite the sentences, correcting errors in the use of negatives.

5. Jason can't go nowhere until he finishes his chores.

_____

6. Before taking this class, Pete didn't know nothing about reptiles.

_____

_____

7. I don't like nothing about insects.

_____

8. Jim doesn't never want to miss a class again.

_____

Conventions: Proofreading

Use proofreading marks to cross out
errors and insert corrections.

Sentence with Errors	Corrected Sentence
Elena's performance was worser than Ralph's.	Elena's performance was **worse** ~~worser~~ than Ralph's.

1–5. Use the proofreading marks to fix the convention
errors in the sentences below.

1. Of the five books I read on mammals, this was the worse.

2. Among the 50 essays submitted, Jose's essay was judged

the better.

3. Of all my grades, my grade in science was the better.

4. Of the three team members, Kara works the faster.

5. Jenna studied more harder than I did.

Focus Trait: Voice
Communicating Feelings

Flat Voice	Interesting Voice
I found a salamander. I was surprised.	I lifted the log. Wow! I was amazed at the bright yellow salamander underneath!

Read each sentence. Rewrite it, giving it interest and feeling.
Write as if you were giving your opinion in a journal entry.

Flat Voice	Interesting Voice
1. My dad and I saw a frog in the pond.	
2. I don't like people throwing things in the pond.	
3. The bullfrogs made funny sounds.	
4. I didn't like holding the toad.	

Name _____ Date _____

Lesson 28
READER'S NOTEBOOK

Museums: Worlds of Wonder
Independent Reading

Museums: Worlds of Wonder

Visit this Museum!

Choose three museums from the selection that you would like to visit. For each museum, reread the section about the museum. Using what you learned about this museum, tell why this museum is important.

Name of Museum	Type of Museum	Why Museum Is Important

Name _____ Date _____

Imagine you visited one of the museums during summer vacation. You want to tell a friend about the great things you saw! Send an e-mail telling your friend what it was like to visit the museum. Make sure to tell your friend why this museum is important.

○ ○ ○   New Message   ⊂⊃

To: _____

From: _____

Subject: You should visit this museum!

_____

_____

_____

_____

_____

_____

_____

_____

_____

_____

_____

_____

_____

Museums: Worlds of Wonder
Spelling: Three-Syllable Words

Three-Syllable Words

Basic 1–11. Write the Basic Word that best replaces the underlined word or words.

Dear Grandma,
Our family (1) <u>trip</u> to Washington, D.C., was great! Mom, Dad, Rick, and I had a good time (2) <u>jointly</u>. We saw (3) <u>a few</u> places, including the (4) <u>building that holds books</u> of Congress. (5) <u>An additional</u> place we visited was the White House. The (6) <u>leader of the United States</u> wasn't there. (7) <u>But</u>, we saw a lot of other things during the tour. For (8) <u>instance</u>, we saw a painting of Abraham Lincoln in the State Dining Room. I wasn't allowed to use my (9) <u>photographic device</u>, or I would have taken pictures for you. My (10) <u>preferred</u> place was the Smithsonian. Washington, D.C., is full of (11) <u>stories from the past</u>.

Love,
Matt

1. _____
2. _____
3. _____
4. _____
5. _____
6. _____
7. _____
8. _____
9. _____
10. _____
11. _____

Challenge 12–13. An astronaut is speaking at your school about her recent shuttle ride through space. You get to talk to the astronaut after her speech. Write a sentence about your talk, using two Challenge Words. Write on a separate sheet of paper.

Spelling Words

Basic
1. library
2. another
3. hospital
4. example
5. deliver
6. history
7. however
8. several
9. vacation
10. important
11. victory
12. imagine
13. camera
14. potato
15. remember
16. together
17. memory
18. favorite
19. continue
20. president

Challenge
internal
ornament
interview
universe
article

Museums: Worlds of Wonder
Spelling: Three-Syllable Words

Word Sort

Write each Basic Word beside the correct heading.

First syllable stressed	**Basic Words:** **Challenge Words:** **Possible Selection Words:**
Second syllable stressed	**Basic Words:** **Challenge Words:** **Possible Selection Words:**

Challenge: Add the Challenge Words to your Word Sort.

Connect to Reading: Look through "Museums: Worlds of Wonder." Find words that have three syllables with first and second syllables stressed. Add them to your Word Sort.

Spelling Words

Basic
1. library
2. another
3. hospital
4. example
5. deliver
6. history
7. however
8. several
9. vacation
10. important
11. victory
12. imagine
13. camera
14. potato
15. remember
16. together
17. memory
18. favorite
19. continue
20. president

Challenge
internal
ornament
interview
universe
article

Proofreading for Spelling

Find the misspelled words and circle them. Write them correctly on the lines below.

In 1906, Hiram Bingham had had enough of studying the histery of the Incas in Peru in the libary at Yale. He knew they were importint to the history of South America for severle reasons. He decided to take a working vacashun to South America. Not wanting to rely on his memery, he took many notes and a kamera so he could remembir all the facts when he went to delivir a speech about his travels.

In 1911, Bingham returned to Peru to lead anether expedition and continew his quest for knowledge about the Incas. One can only imajin his surprise when he discovered Machu Picchu, the "lost city of the Incas." The expedition turned out to be a huge personal victry for Bingham. The ancient stone city, hidden by five hundred years of jungle growth, is considered by some to be the greatest surviving exampel of Incan architecture.

Spelling Words

1. library
2. another
3. hospital
4. example
5. deliver
6. history
7. however
8. several
9. vacation
10. important
11. victory
12. imagine
13. camera
14. potato
15. remember
16. together
17. memory
18. favorite
19. continue
20. president

Challenge

internal
ornament
interview
universe
article

1. _____   8. _____
2. _____   9. _____
3. _____   10. _____
4. _____   11. _____
5. _____   12. _____
6. _____   13. _____
7. _____   14. _____

Possessive Pronouns

- A **possessive pronoun** is a pronoun that shows ownership.
- Possessive pronouns can replace possessive nouns in a sentence.

Possessive Pronouns	
my	its
your	our
her	their
his	

Thinking Questions
Are there possessive nouns in the sentence? Do any of them need to be replaced to avoid repetition?

The teacher gave her students **the students'** tickets to the museum.

The teacher gave her students **their** tickets to the museum.

1–5. **Rewrite each sentence with the correct form of the possessive pronoun in parentheses.**

1. Max and I went to see <u>Max's</u> favorite exhibit. (my, his, our)

_____

2. We observed a dinosaur fossil and read about the <u>fossil's</u> discovery. (our, their, its)

_____

3. We learned about dinosaurs, including <u>dinosaurs'</u> habits and diets. (its, her, their)

_____

4. Mary told me that <u>Mary's</u> brother would love the exhibit, too. (my, her, their)

_____

5. Marcus and I found <u>Marcus's and my</u> class in the museum shop. (its, our, her)

_____

More Possessive Pronouns

Some possessive pronouns are placed before nouns. Others are used by themselves and stand alone.

Thinking Question
Is the possessive pronoun followed by a noun?

Possessive Pronouns that Stand Alone	
mine	hers
yours	ours
his	theirs

The tickets to the exhibit are **ours.**

1–4. **Write the possessive pronoun that stands alone on the line.**

1. Is the ticket to the polar bear exhibit hers? _____

2. The airplane ticket is mine. _____

3. Since we have tickets but cannot attend, would you like to use ours? _____

4. The teacher will give you yours. _____

5–6. **Rewrite each sentence on the line so that the possessive pronoun stands alone.**

5. Which report is your report? _____

6. The report about trees is my report.

_____

Possessive Pronouns

- Some possessive <u>pronouns</u> are placed before <u>nouns</u>.
    Jeff left <u>his</u> <u>backpack</u> on the school bus.
    <u>My</u> <u>books</u> are in Mom's car.
- Other possessive <u>pronouns</u> are used by themselves and stand alone.
    I think the museum tickets are <u>yours</u>.
    The red skates in the locker are <u>mine</u>.

1–6. **Replace the underlined word or words with the correct possessive pronoun.**

1. Jill's inline skates are sitting on <u>Jill's</u> porch. _____

2. "The backpack with reflector strips is <u>my backpack</u>," I said. _____

3. Jane can't find <u>Jane's</u> shoe. _____

4. Which one of the lunches is <u>your lunch</u>? _____

5. The three boys rode <u>the three boys'</u> bikes to school. _____

6. If Ned has my jacket, then I have <u>Ned's jacket</u>. _____

Writing Quotations

- **Quotations** show a speaker's exact words.
- **Capitalize** the first word of a quotation.
- Place **quotation marks** before and after the speaker's exact words.
- Use a **comma** to set off words that tell who is speaking.
- When the quotation comes first, place a **comma** inside the last quotation marks.
- If the quotation is a question or an exclamation, place a **question mark** or **exclamation mark** inside the last quotation marks.

   Ms. Winger said, "Listen to your guide carefully."

1–8. Rewrite the quotations, correcting the punctuation errors.

1. "Have you ever been to the City Museum" asked Chloe.

   _____

2. Yes, I have replied Aiden.

   _____

3. Charlie said "I hope we see dinosaurs".

   _____

4. Marta exclaimed "the Enchanted Caves are so awesome"!

   _____

5. "I like Art City better" said Danielle.

   _____

6. Mr. West suggested "let's go see the World Aquarium now."

   _____

7. This will be fun! exclaimed Sam.

   _____

8. I will have so many things to tell my family, said Luis.

   _____

Name _____ Date _____

Sentence Fluency

To avoid repeated possessive nouns, replace them with possessive pronouns.

Sentence with Repeated Possessive Nouns	Sentence with Possessive Pronouns
Jose wanted <u>Jose's</u> mom to chaperone <u>Jose's</u> field trip to the museum.	Jose wanted <u>his</u> mom to chaperone <u>his</u> field trip to the museum.

1–5. Rewrite each sentence, replacing repeated possessive nouns with possessive pronouns to improve sentence flow.

1. Today, the fourth graders will have fun on <u>the fourth grader's</u> first field trip.

_____

2. Sarah told about <u>Sarah's</u> visit to the museum.

_____

3. Kayla saved a piece of <u>Kayla's</u> favorite cake for <u>Kayla's</u> mother.

_____

4. Pam showed <u>Pam's</u> project to the class.

_____

5. By running in the museum, Tim broke one of the rules that <u>Tim's</u> teacher had given to <u>Tim's</u> class.

_____

Focus Trait: Organization

A well-organized announcement contains:
- a topic or main idea;
- details that support the main idea;
- a sequence of ideas or events that usually happen in order of first, next, and last;
- a conclusion that restates the main idea.

Use a separate sheet of paper. Organize the sentences below in an order that makes sense.

1. Sunday afternoon: Children's concert. Special appearance by Moosy the Cow!

2. Saturday morning, September 27: Family breakfast with the Museum staff

3. Come join the fun. Questions? Call or email the Museum office for more details.

4. Saturday afternoon: Ribbon-cutting ceremony and museum tours

5. Announcing the Gala Opening of the New Children's Museum!

6. Saturday night: Dinner-Dance with raffle. Adults only

7. Save the weekend of September 27–28 so you can enjoy all the activities.

8. Celebrate with your friends and neighbors!

Reader's Guide

Save Timber Woods!

Write a Public Service Announcement

Help neighborhood residents who live near Timber Woods understand the pros and cons of cutting down Timber Woods. Reread pages 49–50 and page 52. Think carefully about Gina's, Laura's, Hector's, and Lucas's arguments on these pages. Use their arguments to fill in the chart below.

CUTTING DOWN TIMBER WOODS	
Pros	**Cons**
1. _____ _____ _____	1. _____ _____ _____
2. _____ _____ _____	2. _____ _____ _____
	3. _____ _____ _____

Write a public service announcement that could be broadcast on local radio or television stations in the characters' neighborhood. Help residents understand the consequences of cutting down Timber Woods. Include five lines of dialogue for the speaker to say. Include two stage directions that let him or her know how to deliver the lines.

Line 1: _____

_____

Line 2: _____

_____

Line 3: _____

_____

Line 4: _____

_____

Line 5: _____

_____

Words with Silent Consonants

Basic 1–10. Write Basic Words on the lines provided that will best complete the sentences.

My aunt's job is to keep the water pipes in people's homes running smoothly. She is a (1) _____. She has to (2) _____ down and work under sinks. Sometimes she has to (3) _____ into small spaces to find the (4) _____ to the plumbing problem. She often has to use tools from her toolbox to (5) _____ pipes together. Working with tools, my aunt has to take care not to scrape a (6) _____ or a wrist. She carries a radio in her toolbox because she likes to (7) _____ to music as she works. The music helps keep her (8) _____ and relaxed as she does her job. Her customers (9) _____ her and praise her work. She says being a plumber is a good, (10) _____ job to have.

Challenge 11–12. You've watched a documentary film about the building of the Egyptian pyramids. Write a review of the film for your class. Use two of the Challenge Words. Write on a separate sheet of paper.

Spelling Words

Basic
1. half
2. comb
3. mortgage
4. honor
5. fasten
6. kneel
7. wreath
8. calm
9. answer
10. handsome
11. wrinkle
12. listen
13. fetch
14. yolk
15. climb
16. honest
17. knuckle
18. plumber
19. limb
20. folktale

Challenge
tomb
glisten
design
hasten
wrestle

Word Sort

Save Timber Woods!
Spelling: Words with Silent Consonants

Write each Basic Word next to the correct heading.

/m/ spelled *mb*	Basic Words: Challenge Words:
/n/ spelled *kn*	Basic Words:
/ô/ spelled *ho*	Basic Words:
/r/ spelled *wr*	Basic Words: Challenge Word:
silent *l, t, d,* or *w*	Basic Words: Challenge Words:
Other silent consonants	Challenge Word:

Challenge: Add the Challenge Words to your Word Sort.

Spelling Words

Basic
1. half
2. comb
3. mortgage
4. honor
5. fasten
6. kneel
7. wreath
8. calm
9. answer
10. handsome
11. wrinkle
12. listen
13. fetch
14. yolk
15. climb
16. honest
17. knuckle
18. plumber
19. limb
20. folktale

Challenge
tomb
glisten
design
hasten
wrestle

Proofreading for Spelling

Save Timber Woods!
Spelling: Words with Silent
Consonants

Find the misspelled words and circle them. Write them
correctly on the lines below.

Spelling Words

1. half
2. comb
3. mortgage
4. honor
5. fasten
6. kneel
7. wreath
8. calm
9. answer
10. handsome
11. wrinkle
12. listen
13. fetch
14. yolk
15. climb
16. honest
17. knuckle
18. plumber
19. limb
20. folktale

Challenge
tomb
glisten
design
hasten
wrestle

After college, Chef Alice Waters went to France,
where she was impressed by the honist food she ate,
from an omelet made with the freshest egg yoke to
fish cooked the day it was caught. She learned that the
French were often willing to spend haff of their income
for quality food products. Since 1971, Alice has owned
Chez Panisse, a California restaurant famous for the
quality of its food. People have been known to komb
the woods and neel in mud beneath the lim of a tree
to fetsh for Alice special foods, such as a mushroom
with an ugly wrinkil and incredible flavor. Other people
grow herbs and make a wreth of them for Alice. She has
worked hard to teach children about growing and eating
fresh food. Today there are children in local schools who
prefer to lisen to Alice talk about gardening than hear a
folktail about a handsum prince.

1. _____
2. _____
3. _____
4. _____
5. _____
6. _____
7. _____
8. _____
9. _____
10. _____
11. _____
12. _____

Using *I* and *me*

- Use the pronoun *I* as the subject of a sentence.
    Eileen and I learned so much!

- Use the pronoun *me* after action verbs and
  after prepositions such as *to, with, for,* or *at.*
    The council gave **David and me** their
    complete attention.
    Will you come with **me** to the meeting?

- When you talk about yourself and another person,
  always name yourself last.

> **Thinking Question**
> *Is the pronoun the
> subject or the object
> of the sentence?*

1–6. Rewrite each sentence with the correct word(s) in parentheses.

1. (Dominic and I, Dominic and me) wanted to save the forest.

   _____

2. Eileen told (I, me) what was happening to the forest.

   _____

3. Carlos and (I, me) realized the deer had nowhere to go.

   _____

4. Deer often visited (me and my family, my family and me).

   _____

5. My brother and (I, me) have seen them look for food.

   _____

6. (He and me, He and I) watched the deer quietly through the window.

   _____

Using the Right Pronoun

- **Subject pronouns** are used as the subject of a sentence. They tell whom or what the sentence is about.
- **Object pronouns** follow action verbs or prepositions such as *to, for, with, in,* or *at.*

Subject Pronouns	Object Pronouns
I, you, he, she, it, we, they	me, you, him, her, it, us, them

We gave the information to **her**, and **she** told **them** about the forestry class.

> **Thinking Questions**
> *Does the pronoun tell who or what does the action? Does the pronoun follow an action verb or the words* to, for, with, in, *or* at?

1–5.   **Rewrite each sentence, using the correct pronoun in parentheses.**

1. Isabel read (we, us) the article about the housing development.

_____

2. Olivia and (he, him) could not believe what they heard.

_____

3. (They, Them) want to cut down huge parts of the forest.

_____

4. To (we, us), the forest should be used for hiking and camping.

_____

5. Since animals cannot speak, we will speak for (them, they).

_____

Reflexive Pronouns

A **reflexive pronoun** is used when the subject and object of a sentence are the same person/thing or people/things. We use reflexive pronouns with the word *by* to mean *alone* or *without help*.

Subject Pronouns		Reflexive Pronouns
I	it	myself
you	we	yourself
he	you (plural)	himself
she	they	herself
		itself
		ourselves
		yourselves
		themselves

I will take care of *myself* someday. *They* like to walk to school *by themselves*.

1–8. Fill in the blanks with the correct reflexive pronoun.

1. When she was hungry, Jane made _____ a sandwich.

2. Be careful, Lisa. Don't cut _____ with the knife.

3. "I think I will build a clubhouse by _____," said Paul.

4. We blamed _____ for getting lost in the museum.

5. Please boys, make _____ feel at home.

6. The girls made five dozen cupcakes by _____.

7. The dog saw _____ in the mirror and barked.

8. Jack made _____ a pizza for lunch.

Commas in Sentences

Use a comma to set off these types of words and phrases:
- the words *yes, no,* and *well* when they begin a sentence
   No, feeding deer human food is not a good idea.
- introductory phrases and clauses
   If you want to see deer, you have to be still.
- the name of a person directly addressed in a sentence.
   Don't blame the deer, Becky, for being hungry.

1–5. Rewrite the sentences, adding commas where they are needed.

1. No I do not want deer in our yard.

_____

2. The poor deer lost their homes Alanna.

_____

3. Well my family is losing our favorite tree.

_____

4. We should get the facts Denzel before we decide.

_____

5. Because we left home late we arrived after the park closed.

_____

6–8. Rewrite the following script. Add three missing commas where they are needed.

Eliot: Well that went better than I expected.
Maria: Eliot you were great!
Gerald: What can we do now to raise money guys?

Sentence Fluency

Name _____ Date _____

Repeating words in writing is uninteresting and awkward.
To avoid using a noun over and over again, replace it
with a pronoun.

Sentence 1	Sentence 2
Caleb didn't like the deer eating his tree.	Caleb scared it away.

Caleb didn't like the deer eating his tree. **He** scared it away.

1–3. Replace the repeated noun with a pronoun to improve sentence fluency.

1.

Sentence 1	Sentence 2
Nicole told her friends about the problem.	Nicole wanted to help.

_____

_____

2.

Sentence 1	Sentence 2
Last year the deer were safer.	The deer had more land.

_____

_____

3.

Sentence 1	Sentence 2
The people of our community have a problem.	The people of our community need to work together.

_____

_____

Focus Trait: Ideas
Focusing on Addressing Objections

Good writers think about how their audience will react to their ideas. In an opinion essay, they try to address any objections ahead of time. This writer addressed the objection by the developer about building houses on Timber Woods.

Opinion: *We should save Timber Woods from being destroyed.*
Possible Objection: *We want to build more houses on the Timber Woods land.*
Revised sentence: *Homes could be built where the Smithfield warehouses are instead of Timber Woods.*

1–3. **Read the idea and the possible objection. Rewrite the sentence so that it addresses the objection. You can refer to "Save Timber Woods!" to find information to answer it.**

1. **Opinion:** Cutting down the forest will cause a lot of problems.

   Possible Objection: It costs too much money for us to buy the land.

   Revised sentence: _____

   _____

2. **Opinion:** Saving the woods is good for the local environment.

   Possible Objection: The woods don't help the town in any way.

   Revised sentence: _____

   _____

3. **Opinion:** Wildlife creatures belong in their natural environments.

   Possible Objection: It's nice to see deer in my backyard.

   Revised sentence: _____

   _____

Mystery at Reed's Pond

Create a Web Page

Help the Pond Patrol complete their science log. Then, help them draw conclusions about invasive species based on what they saw and learned. Reread page 71 for information about invasive species from Mr. Roberts to help fill in Pond Patrol's log.

SCIENCE LOG		
Details	**What I Learned**	**Conclusions about Invasive Species**
1. A western turtle used to live in the pond. Now there is a red-eared slider turtle there.	_____ _____ _____ _____ _____	_____ _____ _____ _____ _____
2. A nest is crushed and is missing eggs.	_____ _____ _____ _____ _____	_____ _____ _____ _____ _____

Write the text for a web page from an environmental site informing people about the threats of invasive species. Using what you learned, explain the dangers of introducing a new species to an area.

File Edit View Favorites Tools Help

Address e

The Center for Information on Invasive Species

The Dangers of Invasive Species

_____
_____
_____
_____
_____
_____
_____

Unusual Spellings

Mystery at Reed's Pond
Spelling: Unusual Spellings

Basic 1–10.
Complete
the puzzles
by writing the
Basic Word for
each clue.

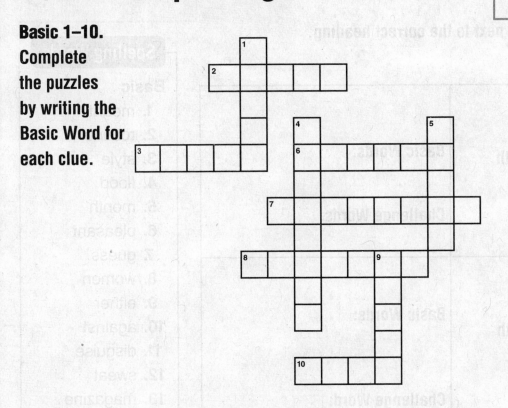

Spelling Words

Basic

1. meant
2. routine
3. style
4. flood
5. month
6. pleasant
7. guess
8. women
9. either
10. against
11. disguise
12. sweat
13. magazine
14. guard
15. receive
16. wonder
17. league
18. type
19. ceiling
20. money

Challenge

plaid
onion
guarantee
rhyme
submarine

Across

2. to form an opinion without being sure

3. to fill or cover with water

6. a group working toward a common goal

7. a weekly or monthly publication

8. in contact with

10. a group sharing common traits

Down

1. someone who watches over or protects

4. enjoyable or attractive

5. past of "to have as its meaning"

9. a way of doing something

Challenge 11–12. Create two book titles: one about a trip to the ocean bottom in a colorful vessel and one about a collection of humorous poetry. Use two of the Challenge Words. Write on a separate sheet of paper.

Name _____ Date _____

Word Sort

Write each Basic Word next to the correct heading.

Mystery at Reed's Pond
Spelling: Unusual Spellings

Unusual Spellings with One Syllable
Basic Words:
Challenge Words:

Unusual Spellings with Two Syllables
Basic Words:
Challenge Word:

Unusual Spellings with Three Syllables
Basic Words:
Challenge Words:

Challenge: Add the Challenge Words to your Word Sort.

Spelling Words

Basic
1. meant
2. routine
3. style
4. flood
5. month
6. pleasant
7. guess
8. women
9. either
10. against
11. disguise
12. sweat
13. magazine
14. guard
15. receive
16. wonder
17. league
18. type
19. ceiling
20. money

Challenge
plaid
onion
guarantee
rhyme
submarine

Name _____ Date _____

Proofreading for Spelling

Find the misspelled words and circle them. Write them correctly on the lines below.

I was following my rootine for the munth, practicing with the bowling leegue after work. I'm an amateur detective, so I gess I'm always on the lookout for trouble. I arrived at the bowling alley early, and I noticed two strange womin. I couldn't help but wonnder if ether of them was the tipe to bowl. I didn't think so. The tall one wore a disgize. I looked up and began to swet with fear. There was a figure hanging from the seiling. I turned to run.

The tall woman leaned right agenst my face. "You can't go," she said. "I didn't recieve my monie yet." Shaking, I asked her what she ment. She laughed and told me she needed to be paid for the mystery party. Then I realized the figure was just a decoration. It's a good thing I'm just an *amateur* detective.

Spelling Words

Basic
1. meant
2. routine
3. style
4. flood
5. month
6. pleasant
7. guess
8. women
9. either
10. against
11. disguise
12. sweat
13. magazine
14. guard
15. receive
16. wonder
17. league
18. type
19. ceiling
20. money

Challenge
plaid
onion
guarantee
rhyme
submarine

1. _____   9. _____

2. _____   10. _____

3. _____   11. _____

4. _____   12. _____

5. _____   13. _____

6. _____   14. _____

7. _____   15. _____

8. _____

Pronoun Contractions

- Pronouns can be combined with some verbs to form **contractions**.
- An **apostrophe** replaces the letter or letters that are left out.

    I'm going to study that turtle until **it's** engraved in my memory.

- Contractions for the pronouns *he, she,* and *it,* when used with the verbs *is* and *has,* are the same (*he's, she's, it's*).

Thinking Question
What two words can I combine to make a contraction?

1–5.   On the line, write the contraction for the underlined words.

1. <u>We are</u> observing nature with our class. _____

2. <u>They have</u> taken many notes about the pond. _____

3. <u>You will</u> have time to observe everything. _____

4. Adrian said <u>he had</u> never seen a turtle like that. _____

5. <u>You are</u> responsible for your actions. _____

6–10.   On the line, write the two words that make up each underlined contraction.

6. Lea thinks <u>we've</u> solved the mystery. _____

7. What do you think <u>they'll</u> do with the red turtles? _____

8. <u>You've</u> seen the boy put the red turtle in the pond. _____

9. Mr. Roberts says that <u>it's</u> important to take care of the pond. _____

10. <u>I've</u> done enough research on turtles to know that this answer is wrong.

_____

Pronouns and Homophones

• **Homophones** are words that sound alike but have different spellings and meanings. Some pronoun contractions are homophones.

Homophones	Meaning
it's	it is
its	belonging to it, of it
they're	they are
their	belonging to them
there	in that place
you're	you are
your	belonging to you

Thinking Question
What sentence clues can I use to figure out the meaning and correct spelling of the homophone?

You're very kind to animals and their habitats.
They're enjoying your book on turtles.

1–6. **Read each sentence. Write the correct homophone in parentheses.**

1. We found a cracked egg (their, there). _____

2. The egg should have been in (it's, its) nest. _____

3. (They're, There) observing the young turtles in the pond. _____

4. (Your, You're) correct about the effects of pollution. _____

5. (Your, You're) computer gave us the information we needed. _____

6. (Its, It's) hard to believe that the boy did not want to keep his pet turtles.

_____

Using Pronouns

- Pronouns can be combined with some verbs to form contractions.
- An apostrophe replaces the letter or letters that are left out.
    Example: I am = I'm
- Contractions for *he, she,* and *it* when used with verbs *is* and *has* are the same.
    Example: he is = he's   he has = he's
- Some pronoun contractions are homophones.
    Example: it's = it is   its = belonging to it

1–5.   On the line, write the contraction for the underlined words.

1. <u>I am</u> ready to write a report about my field trip.

_____

2. My teacher says that <u>I will</u> have one week to finish it.

_____

3. Sylvia said <u>she has</u> decided to do a photo essay as her report.

_____

4. She said that <u>it is</u> going to be her best report ever.

_____

5. Les thinks <u>we are</u> going to have fun reading our reports in class.

_____

6–10.   On the line, write the correct homophone for each sentence.

6. (Your, You're) going to visit the science museum next week.

_____

7. (There, Their) will be students from the whole school district at the museum.

_____

8. (Their, They're) going on the same guided tour as your class.

_____

9. (It's, Its) going to be an amazing experience!

_____

10. Don't forget to bring (you're, your) cameras.

_____

Commas in Sentences

- A **series** is a list of three or more items with the word *and* or *or* before the last item.
- Use *commas* to separate the items in a series. Put a comma after each item except the last one.
- Some choppy sentences can be combined using a series.

    Snakes and lizards are reptiles. So are

    alligators and crocodiles.

    Snakes, lizards, turtles, alligators, and

    crocodiles are all reptiles.

- Use a comma to separate the **month and date from the year.**
- Use a comma to separate a **city or town and its state.**

    I will be sixteen on August 4, 2010.

    The best park is in Yellowstone, Montana.

1–5.   Rewrite the sentences, adding commas where they are needed.

1. The scales of a snake are cool dry and hard.

_____

2. This park was opened on July 4 1949.

_____

3. A turtle in danger can pull its head legs and tail into its shell.

_____

4. Most turtles live in ponds lakes rivers or the ocean.

_____

5. Next summer I'm going to ecology camp in Orlando Florida.

_____

6.   Combine the sentences using a series. Write the new sentence on the lines.

Both turtles and tortoises bask in the sun. They both have bony shells. Turtles and tortoises can withdraw inside their shells for protection.

_____

_____

Conventions: Proofreading

Sentence with Errors	Corrected Sentence
Im sure their excited to have solved the mystery.	I'm sure they're excited to have solved the mystery.

1–6. Use the proofreading marks to fix the convention errors in the sentences below.

1. Ive never solved a mystery before.

2. Its about time we helped animals by saving their habitats.

3. Youd never guess what my favorite pond animal is.

4. I love frogs because their so interesting.

5. Youll be glad that you did so much to help.

6. The western pond turtle is being squeezed out of it's habitat.

Focus Trait: Sentence Fluency Using Different Kinds of Sentences

Writers can give the same information in different kinds of sentences.

The western pond turtle needs to have its home protected.

Question: Doesn't the western pond turtle deserve a safe home?

Exclamation: The western pond turtle must have a safe home!

1–3. Rewrite each sentence as the type indicated.

1. If we work together, we can save the animals at Reed's Pond.

Command: _____

Question: _____

2. The red-eared slider should not be released in Reed's Pond.

Exclamation: _____

Command: _____

3. Saving the pond's native species is very important.

Question: _____

Exclamation: _____

